W9-AGD-166

mustsees
LAS VEGAS

© JUPITERIMAGES/ Creatas / Alamy

Editorial Director	Cynthia Clayton Ochterbeck
mustsees Las Vegas	
Editor	Jonathan P. Gilbert
Principal Writer	Lark Ellen Gould
Production Manager	Natasha G. George
Cartography	Peter Wrenn
Photo Editor	Jonathan P. Gilbert, Yoshimi Kanazawa
Proofreader	Alison Coupe
Layout	Chris Bell, Natasha G. George
Cover & Interior Design	Chris Bell
Contact Us:	Michelin Maps and Guides
	One Parkway South
	Greenville, SC 29615
	USA
	www.michelintravel.com
	michelin.guides@us.michelin.com
	Michelin Maps and Guides
	Hannay House
	39 Clarendon Road
	Watford, Herts WD17 1JA
	UK
	☏ (01923) 205 240
	www.ViaMichelin.com
	travelpubsales@uk.michelin.com
Special Sales:	For information regarding bulk sales, customized editions and premium sales, please contact our Customer Service Departments:

USA	1-800-432-6277
UK	(01923) 205 240
Canada	1-800-361-8236

Michelin Apa Publications Ltd
A joint venture between Michelin and Langenscheidt

58 Borough High Street, London SE1 1XF, United Kingdom

No part of this publication may be reproduced in any form without the prior permission of the publisher.

© 2009 Michelin Apa Publications Ltd
ISBN 978-1-906261-61-0
Printed: December 2008
Printed and bound: Himmer, Germany

Note to the reader:
While every effort is made to ensure that all information printed in this guide is correct and up-to-date, Michelin Apa Publications Ltd. accepts no liability for any direct, indirect or consequential losses howsoever caused so far as such can be excluded by law. Admission prices listed for sights in this guide are for a single adult, unless otherwise specified.

Caesars Palace

Garden of the Gods, Caesars Palace

Introduction

Las Vegas: The Neon Jungle

Must See

p 82

Must Do

Michelin Guide

Must Know

TABLE OF CONTENTS

★★★ATTRACTIONS

Unmissable attractions awarded three stars in this guide include:

Bellagio p 22

Death Valley National Park p 94

Wynn Las Vegas p 24

Grand Canyon National Park p 91

MUST KNOW

The Venetian p 23

The Strip p 20

Springs Preserve p 80

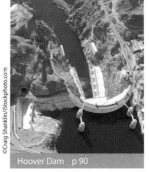
Hoover Dam p 90

★★★ ATTRACTIONS

Unmissable sights in and around Vegas

For more than 75 years people have used the Michelin stars to take the guesswork out of travel. Our star-rating system helps you make the best decision on where to go, what to do, and what to see.

★★★	Absolutely Must See
★★	Really Must See
★	Must See
No Star	See

MUST KNOW

🐻 ACTIVITIES

Unmissable Vegas shows, restaurants and more
For every Vegas casino and stunning Grand Canyon vista there are a thousand more activities. We recommend every activity in this guide, but our top picks are highlighted with the Michelin Man logo.

Remember to Look-out for the Michelin Man for the top activities.

See the red tabbed section for Michelin Guide addresses.

STAR ATTRACTIONS

CALENDAR OF EVENTS

Listed below is a selection of Las Vegas' most -popular annual events. Please note that dates may change from year to year. For more detailed information, contact the Las Vegas Convention and Visitors Authority: 702-892-0711; www.lvcva.com.

January
Martin Luther King, Jr. Parade
Downtown Las Vegas
(702) 440-6400
www.kingweeklasvegas.com

February
Chinese New Year Celebration
Chinatown Plaza, 4255 Spring
Mountain Rd. 702-221-8448
www.lvchinatown.com

March
St. Patrick's Celebration
Fremont St. 702-678-5777
www.vegasexperience.com

April
Mardi Gras Festival
Fremont St. 702-678-5777
www.vegasexperience.com
Helldorado Days
Rodeo Western Fest
Thomas and Mack Center
702-739-3267
www.thomasandmack.com

Clark County Fair and Rodeo
Fairgrounds in Logondale
888-876-FAIR
www.ccfair.com

May
International Food
and Folklife Festival
Clark County Government
Center Amphitheater
702-455-8200
www.accessclarkcounty.com
Cinco de Mayo Festival
Lorenzi Park, W. Washington St.
702-284-6400

June
Jazz Festival
Fremont St.
702-678-5777
www.lasvegasjazzfestival.com
CineVegas
Las Vegas Strip
888-8VEGAS8
www.cinevegas.com

December: New Year's Eve in Vegas

©Barry J. Holmes/Lamoine Photo/Fremont Street Experience

September

San Gennaro Street Fair
Flamingo Rd. Valley View Blvd.
702-286-4944
www.sangennarofeast.net

Mexican Independence Day
Lorenzi Park, W. Washington St.
702-284-6400

Greek Food Festival
St. John's Greek Orthodox
Church. 702-248-3896

Ho'olaule'a Pacific Island Festival
Lorenzi Park, W. Washington St.
702-382-6939
http://lvhcc.org/hoolaulea

Taste of Vegas
Clark County Desert Breeze Park
8275 W. Spring Mountain Rd.
702-243-5922, 702-455-8200
www.tasteofvegas.com

Oktoberfest
German-American Club of
America, 1110 E. Lake Mead
Blvd. 702-649-8503

October

Jaycee State Fair
Cashman Field, Las Vegas
Blvd. N. at Washington St.
702-386-7100

Art in the Park
Bicentennial Park, Boulder City
702-294-1611
www.artinthepark.org

Renaissance Festival
Sunset Park, 2601 E. Sunset Rd.
702-455-8200
www.lvrenfair.com

Las Vegas Basque Festival
Lorenzi Park, W. Washington St.
702-361-6458

November

Professional Bullriders
World Finals
Thomas & Mack Center
University of Nevada, Las Vegas
www.pbrnow.com

October Renaissance Festival

©Las Vegas Renaissance Festival

Miss Chinatown Las Vegas
Chinatown Plaza
4255 Spring Mountain Rd.
702-221-8448
www.lvchinatown.com

Steve Powers Great
Las vegas Craft Show
Cashman Center
www.stevepowers.com

December

National Finals Rodeo
Thomas & Mack Center
University of Nevada, Las Vegas
888-637-7633
www.nfr-rodeo.com

International Gem
& Jewelry Show
Cashman Center
301-294-1640
www.intergem.net

New Year's Eve in Vegas
Fremont St. 702-678-5777
www.las-vegas-new-years-
eve.com
Las Vegas Convention & Visitors
Authority 702-892-0711

PRACTICAL INFORMATION

WHEN TO GO

If you can't take the heat, stay out of the oven—known as Las Vegas—from June until October. With an average of 307 sunny days a year, the city usually sees only four inches of rain annually—September is the rainiest month, though some locals swear it is July. Granted, you won't find the humidity (average 29%) here that you do in other parts of the country. Still, Las Vegas sits in the middle of the Mojave Desert and summers can see temperatures climbing as high as 120°F during the day and only dropping 20 degrees at night. Spring and autumn are milder with daytime temperatures averaging in the 70s. In the winter, temperatures may drop below freezing, although the average high is between 50–60°F. If you hate crowds, don't come during national holidays, especially when there's a three-day weekend involved. Certain conventions and events also bring in huge numbers of people, raising rates sky-high. From late February to early May, and then again from mid-September to mid-November, Las Vegas is simply divine. Bring a good pair of walking shoes or even hiking boots because you will want to be outside, whether that means walking The Strip (see p26) or hiking the desert. Pool poppers will want to check ahead with the hotel to make sure there is a four-season soaking spot on the premises. The least crowded time to hit The Strip is traditionally the week or two before Christmas through a day or two before New Year's Eve. The buffet lines are at their shortest and the hotels roll out some of their best promotions during that time. However, because of recent declines in visitor numbers due to rising gas prices and reduced air traffic, visitors will be amazed to find how affordable a mid-week stay at a top Strip property can be no matter what the season.

KNOW BEFORE YOU GO

Useful Websites
www.visitlasvegas.com - Official tourism website of Las Vegas.
www.lasvegasadvisor.com - Vegas expert Anthony Curtis gives the inside eye on Vegas's top spots.
www.vegas.com - An easy to navigate and up-to-date travel site.
www.lasvegas.com - From hotels to gambling, it all starts here.

Visitor Information
Before you go, check with the following organizations to obtain the *Las Vegas Official Visitor Guide*, as well as maps and information on accommodations, dining, shopping, festivals and recreation:

Average Seasonal Temperatures in Las Vegas			
	Jan	**Apr**	**July**	**Oct**
Avg. High	57°F/14°C	78°F/26°C	104°F/40°C	81°F/27°C
Avg. Low	34°F/1°C	44°F/7°C	68°F/20°C	46°F/8°C

Las Vegas
Visitor Information Center
Operated by the Las Vegas Convention & Visitors Authority
3150 Paradise Road, Las Vegas, NV 89109
702-892-0711; www.lvcva.com
Open year-round daily 8am–5pm

Las Vegas
Chamber of Commerce
3720 Howard Hughes Parkway
Las Vegas, NV 89109
702-735-1616; www.lvchamber.com

International Visitors
In addition to the tourism offices throughout Nevada, visitors from outside the US can obtain information from the website of the Las Vegas Convention and Visitors Authority *(www.lvcva.com)* or from the US embassy or consulate in their country of residence. For a complete list of American consulates and embassies abroad, visit the website for the Department of State, Bureau of Consular Affairs *(http://USembassy.gov)*.

Entry Requirements – Travelers entering the United States under the Visa Waiver Program (VWP) must present a machine-readable passport to enter the US without a visa; otherwise, a US visa is required. Required entry documents must include biometric identifiers (fingerscans—full Visa Waiver Program requirements can be found at http://travel.state.gov). Citizens of countries participating in the VWP are permitted to enter the US for general business or tourism for up to 90 days without a visa. For a list of countries participating in the VWP, contact the US consulate in your country of residence. Citizens of non-participating countries

must have a visa. Upon entry, non-resident foreign visitors must present a valid passport and round-trip ticket. As of December 31, 2006, travelers to and from Canada must present a passport or other secure, accepted document to enter or re-enter the US. Inoculations are generally not required, but check with the US embassy or consulate. All citizens of non-VWP-participating countries must have a visitor's visa.

US Customs – All articles brought into the US must be declared at the time of entry. Prohibited items include plant material, firearms and ammunition (if not for sporting purposes), meat/poultry products. For other prohibited items, exemptions and information, contact the US embassy or consulate before departing, or the US Customs Service *(877-287-8667; www.customs.treas.gov)*.

Accessibility
Disabled Travelers – Federal law requires that businesses (including hotels and restaurants) provide access for the disabled, devices for the hearing impaired and designated parking spaces.
For information, contact the Society for Accessible Travel and Hospitality (SATH): 347 Fifth Ave., Suite 610, New York NY 10016 *(212-447-7284; www.sath.org)*.
All national parks have facilities for the disabled and offer free or discounted passes *(National Park Service, Office of Public Inquiries, P.O. Box 37127, Room 1013, Washington, DC 20013-7127; 202-208-4747; www.nps.gov)*.
Passengers who will need assistance with train or bus travel should give advance notice to

Amtrak *(800-872-7245 or 800-523-6590/TDD; www.amtrak.com)* or Greyhound *(800-752-4841 or 800-345-3109/TDD; www.greyhound.com)*. Make reservations for hand-controlled rental cars in advance with the rental company.

Senior Citizens – Many hotels, attractions and restaurants offer discounts to visitors age 62 or older (proof of age may be required). The **AARP** (formerly the American Association of Retired Persons) at 601 E St. NW, Washington, DC 20049 *(888-687-2277; www.aarp.com)* offers discounts to its members.

GETTING THERE

By Air
McCarran International Airport (LAS), located 4 miles southeast of The Strip, handles domestic and international flights *(5757 Wayne Newton Blvd.; 702-261-5743; www.mccarran.com)*. Information desks or kiosks are located throughout the airport. **Shuttles and taxis** can be found outside door 11 in the baggage-claim area. Bel-Trans shuttles leave every 10 minutes *($6 to Strip hotels, $7.50 to off-Strip hotels; reservations: 739-7990 or 800-274-7433)*. Taxis to Strip hotels average $10–$20 *(cash only)*. There's a consolidated **car-rental depot** located off-site; you can catch one of the many continuous buses to the lot where 11 car companies have rental desks. The **Ground Transportation Center** near baggage claim has information about shuttles, car rentals and limousine transport.

By Bus
There is no Amtrak train service to Las Vegas, but you can get there by bus. The **Greyhound** bus station is located downtown *(200 S. Main St.; 702-384-9561 or 800-231-2222; www.greyhound.com)*.

By Car
Direct interstate access to Las Vegas is via I-15, which runs between Butte, Montana and San Diego, California.
Driving in the US – Visitors bearing valid driver's licenses issued by their country of residence are not required to obtain an International Driver's License. However, drivers must carry vehicle registration and/or rental contract, and proof of automobile insurance at all times. Gasoline is sold by the gallon. Vehicles in the US are driven on the right-hand side of the road.

GETTING AROUND

Walking The Strip
The Las Vegas Strip *(Las Vegas Blvd.)* is 3.5 miles long, running, in the south, from Russell Road (by Mandalay Bay) to Charleston Boulevard, to the north, then on to downtown. To get your bearings, you need to know that The Strip is crossed by five major streets: Russell, Tropicana, Flamingo, Spring Mountain and Sahara. Overhead walkways connect several properties: New York-New York, the MGM Grand, the Tropicana and Excalibur over the junction of Las Vegas Blvd. and Tropicana Ave.; Caesars Palace, Bellagio and Bally's over the junction of Las Vegas Blvd. and Flamingo Rd.; The Venetian to TI over Las Vegas Blvd.; and Wynn Las Vegas to

Car Rental		
Car Rental Company	**Reservations**	**Internet**
Alamo	800-327-9633	www.alamo.com
Avis	800-331-1212	www.avis.com
Budget	800-527-0700	www.drivebudget.com
Dollar	800-800-4000	www.dollar.com
Enterprise	800-325-8007	www.enterprise.com
Hertz	800-654-3131	www.hertz.com
National	800-227-7368	www.nationalcar.com
Thrifty	800-331-4200	www.thrifty.com

Fashion Show Mall over Las Vegas Blvd. at Spring Mountain Rd.

By Bus
Double-decker Deuce buses run from the Downtown Transportation Center *(Stewart Ave. & Casino Center Blvd.)* down The Strip past Mandalay Bay and the Four Seasons about every 8 to 17 minutes depending on time of day, 24 hours a day, seven days a week, stopping at designated bus stops deemed popular for visitors. Buses to The Strip are $2 one way; pay when you get on *(exact change required)*. Buses off The Strip are $1.25 each way *(exact change required)*. Timetables for the Citizen Area Transit buses (CAT), which go all over the city, are available on buses and in the hotels. *(For routes and schedules: 702-228-7433 or www.rtcsouthernnevada.com)*.

By Taxi
Taxis line up outside all hotel entrances. Cabs cannot be hailed on the street; summon them at cab stands or by calling the cab company.

By Trolley
The **Las Vegas Strip Trolley** runs to specified hotels every 20 minutes. The white-and-green trolleys operate daily from 8:30am–midnight, including holidays *($2.50 one ride per loop–three loops: Downtown, North Strip and South Strip, exact change required; All day passes: $4.25. Call 702-382-1404, www.striptrolley.com)*. Trolleys serve the vast majority of hotels on The Strip, from Mandalay Bay to the Stratosphere.

By Monorail
The **Las Vegas Monorail** *(www.lvmonorail.com)* stops at 11 hotel-resort properties on The Strip and less directly connects passengers with another 16. It begins its 4-mile, 14-minute north-south run at the Sahara Hotel *(Sahara Ave.)* and ends up at the MGM Grand *(Tropicana Ave.)*. Fares are $5 one-way, and $15 for a one-day pass, although discounted promotions and packages are available and noted on the website. The route, with stops at the Las Vegas Hilton, the Convention Center, Wynn, Harrah's/Imperial Palace, Flamingo/

15

Caesars Palace and Bally's/Paris, and MGM Grand, runs parallel to The Strip behind the hotels and offers great views of the backlots. Note that the walk from the monorail platform to the casino or The Strip is usually a long one.

By Car

Don't drive unless you know the back entrances to the hotels and can avoid The Strip, which tends to be gridlocked at all hours. All The Strip hotels have valet parking *(standard tip for valet attendants is $1–2)*. The speed limit on The Strip is 35mph; seatbelts must be worn at all times.

BASIC INFORMATION

Accommodations

For a list of suggested accommodations, see Hotels.

For the best deal, book your room in advance. Room rates are dependent on occupancy; the higher the occupancy at a property, the more the rooms will cost. For that reason, prices fluctuate from day to day (sometimes even within the same day). At certain times of the year, it's possible to get a luxury hotel room or suite at a budget price, or you might end up paying top prices for a low-rent room. As a rule of thumb, prices are lower during the week and in low-occupancy months (traditionally during the summer and in January). Rates are highest at hotels on The Strip, but the convenience of being near the action is worth the extra cost. Rooms downtown, and especially off The Strip, will be quieter and less expensive.

Las Vegas Convention & Visitors Authority Reservation Service: *800-332-5333.*

Campgrounds are available at Mt. Charleston, Dolomite Campgrounds and Kyle Canyon Campgrounds; all are run by the U.S. Forest Service's Spring Mountains National Recreation division *(702-515-5400; www.fs.fed.us)*. There is also camping in Red Rock Canyon *(702-363-1921; www.redrockcanyonlv.org)*.

RV Parks in Las Vegas have full hook-ups and accept pets. Rates generally run less than $20 a night. Reservations are recommended.

California RV Park – *Stewart Ave. at Main St. 702-385-1222 or 800-634-6505.*

Circus Circus KOA Park – *500 Circus Circus Dr. 702-733-9707, or 800-562-7270.*

KOA Las Vegas – *4315 Boulder Hwy. 702-451-5527 or 800-562-7782.*

The Ranch Experience

If you have a hankering for some Old West cattle roping, camping out, or riding off into the sunset (often with a campfire dinner), here are some places to contact:

Sagebrush Ranch
702-256-6049
Cowboy Trail Rides
702-387-2457
Bonnie Springs Ranch
702-875-4191
Mt. Charleston Riding Stables
702-387-2457

Property	Phone/Website	Property	Phone/Website
Best Western	800-528-1234 www.bestwestern.com	**Hyatt**	800-233-1234 www.hyatt.com
Comfort, Clarion & Quality Inns	800-228-5150 www.comfortinn.com	**ITT Sheraton**	800-325-3535 www.sheraton.com
Crowne Plaza	800-227-6963 www.crowneplaza.com	**Marriott**	800-228-9290 www.marriott.com
Days Inn	800-325-2525 www.daysinn.com	**Ramada**	800-228-2828 www.ramada.com
Hilton	800-445-8667 www.hilton.com	**Ritz-Carlton**	800-241-3333 www.ritzcarlton.com
Holiday Inn	800-465-4329 www.holiday-inn.com	**Westin**	800-937-8461 www.westin.com

Major hotel and motel chains with locations in Las Vegas include:

Business Hours

Many services run 24-hours. These include grocery stores, drug stores, gas stations, coffee shops, wedding chapels and much more (you can even find laudramats and hair salons open in the midnight hours). Casinos and many of their restaurants, bars and nightclubs run all hours, as do their bank cages. Government offices and bank offices have standard daytime hours: an exception is the wedding license bureau downtown, which is open 8 am–midnight every day of the week.

Communications

Telephones – Most hotels will charge a fee for all phone calls made from the guestroom, so it is best to use a mobile. High-speed WiFi is available in most hotel rooms for a charge of around $13 per day, and is often free in convention and conferences areas.

Important Phone Numbers	
(24hrs)	
Police (non-emergency)	311
Medical Services: House Call USA	800-468-3537
24-hour Pharmacies:	
Walgreens, 1101 Las Vegas Blvd. S	702-471-6844
Sav-On, 3250 Las Vegas Blvd.	702-643-8538
Poison Control Center, Clark County	800-446-6179
Time (commercial information service)	702-853-1212

It's Showtime!

At Vegas casinos, showtimes, prices and dark days (nights when the show isn't playing) will often change, so call the hotel box office to get up-to-date information.

To reach another Las Vegas hotel from the casino you are in, simply pick up a house phone located near the bank of public phones and dial zero. Hotel operators are usually willing to oblige.

Area codes – To make a long-distance call, dial: 1+area code+seven-digit number.
Las Vegas Area: 702.

Discounts

Discounts are delivered to coupon rippers, newsletter subscribers and slot players. Coupon pages exist in nearly all the top throw-away publications such as What's On, Las Vegas 24/7, LVM and all manner of print that can be grabbed from visitors centers, taxi cabs and concierge desks. Find $2 to 20 percent discounts for anything from a breakfast buffet to a 'copter ride to the Grand Canyon. A top spot to check is LasVegasAdvisor.com. There are promos to be found as well as a handy Las Vegas deals book that comes with a newsletter subscription. The site specializes in keeping up with the best deals in town. Joining a "players club" and playing for points at your favorite casino is the best and quickest way to rack up freebies.

Discount passes – The Las Vegas Explorer Pass can bring significant savings to those who want an active see-and-do trip to Sin City. For a pre-paid cost of $70 to $170, the bearer gets a credit card-sized pass and admission to up to five major attractions plus a host of other discounts *(866-794-5227; www.explorerpass.com/lasvegas)*.

Electricity

Voltage in the US is 120 volts AC, 60 Hz. Foreign-made appliances may need AC adapters (available at specialty travel and electronics stores) as well as North American flat-blade plugs.

Media

Newspapers and Magazines – Consult the city's major daily newspaper, the *Las Vegas Review Journal (www.reviewjournal.com)*, for dining and entertainment news. You'll also learn what's happening in *Nevada Magazine*.

Money

Currency Exchange – Exchange currency at downtown banks and McCarran Airport. For cash transfers use Western Union *(800-325-6000; www.westernunion.com)*.

Cash and Cheques – US banks, stores, restaurants and hotels accept traveler's checks with picture identification.

Lost and Stolen -
American Express, *800-528-4800*
Diners Club, *800-234-6377*
MasterCard, 800-307-7309
VISA, *800-336-8472*

What's On in Vegas?

Try these useful websites:
www.lasvegas-nv.com
www.lasvegas24hours.com
www.lvol.com
www.Vegas.com
www.a2zlasvegas.com

Measurement Equivalents									
Degrees Fahrenheit	95°	86°	77°	68°	59°	50°	41°	32°	23°	14°
Degrees Celsius	35°	30°	25°	20°	15°	10°	5°	0°	-5°	-10°

1 inch = 2.5 centimeters	1 foot = 30.5 centimeters
1 mile = 1.6 kilometers	1 pound = 0.4 kilograms
1 quart = 0.9 liters	1 gallon = 3.8 liters

Smoking

A law passed in 2006 set up a smoking ban in Las Vegas anywhere near the serving of food. That means all restaurants and most indoor public spaces are now smoke free. Casinos remain untouched by the laws.

Sports

Yes, there is life after gaming and much of it is outdoors. From golf, tennis and cycling to boating at Lake Mead, rock climbing at Red Rock Canyon, or skiing on Mt. Charleston, there's no lack of things to do.

Boxing – Las Vegas has become a boxing mecca with championship fights held at the MGM Grand, Mandalay Bay, Caesars Palace and Wynn Las Vegas. Ringside seats can cost as much as $1,500 while the "cheap" seats go for $100–$200.

Car Racing – A 1,500-acre motorsports complex, **Las Vegas Motor Speedway** *(7000 Las Vegas Blvd. N.; 702-644-4444; www.lvms.com)*, can accommodate up to 107,000 spectators. Highlights include the annual UAW-DaimlerChrysler 400 *(Mar)*, and the National Hot Rod Association drag-racing events *(Apr & Oct)*.

College Sports – Fans can watch the University of Las Vegas Runnin' Rebels play football and basketball *(campus bordered by Maryland Pkwy., Tropicana Ave., Paradise Rd & Flamingo Rd.)*. Basketball games are held at the Thomas & Mack Center *(4505 Maryland Pkwy.)*. Catch football matches at Sam Boyd Stadium *(7000 Russell Rd.)*. Tickets: 702-739-3267 or www.unlvtickets.com.

Golf – Las Vegas currently boasts more than 50 golf courses, designed by such big-name players as Arnold Palmer, Robert Trent Jones Sr., and Pete Dye. For websites with up-to-the-minute information, reviews and tee time booking capabilities, try *www.las vegasgolf.com* and *www.lasvegas golfcourses.com.*

Rodeo – Every year, the National Finals Rodeo (NFR) comes to town in December and the Professional Bull Riders World Finals happen in November. *(702-895-3900; www. nfr-rodeo.com)*.

Taxes

Prices displayed do not include sales tax (7.75% in Las Vegas), which is not reimbursable.

Time

Las Vegas operates on Pacific Standard Time.

Tipping

It is customary to give waiters 15–20% of the sum, porters $1 per bag, chamber maids $1 per day, and cab drivers 15% of the fare.

PRACTICAL INFORMATION

19

LAS VEGAS

Planet Vegas? You could say Las Vegas is, indeed, in its own orbit… in an eternal elipse around all that piques desire, heats up nagging appetites and satisfies with a certain punch that leaves one longing for more. Las Vegas is not just a whirling burst of neon welling from the desert dust, nor a spectre of blinding glass towers filing down a seemingly endless canyon of color and motion. It is more than seductive blue swimming pools, costume crazy entertainment and oceans of green felt. Vegas is a state of mind. To reach it you must leave your daily concerns and step into a land beyond time. Prepare yourself for the G-factor: Glitz, glitter, glamour, gee-whiz and gold—the new standard in luxury. Traveler's tip: Hang on and don't look back.

Set in Las Vegas Valley, surrounded by mountain ranges and, just beyond, by the forbidding sands of the Mojave Desert, Las Vegas has gone from being a quiet spot in the desert to a world-class resort destination. The city's history is quite a colorful one. Twelve thousand years ago or so, Las Vegas was a marsh covered with lush vegetation. As eon after eon passed, the marsh receded and the rivers disappeared. What remained was an arid, parched landscape that could nurture only the hardiest of plants and animals. Water trapped underground in the geological strata of the Las Vegas Valley sporadically surfaced to nourish the plants, creating an oasis in the desert as the life-giving water flowed to the Colorado River. Protected from discovery by the harsh desert that surrounded it, the site that would become Las Vegas was hidden for centuries from all but isolated tribes of Native Americans.

On Christmas Day in 1829, a Mexican trader, named **Antonio Armijo**, was leading a 60-man party along the Spanish Trail to Los Angeles when he veered from the usual route. While his caravan was

resting about 100 miles northeast of present-day Vegas, a scouting party rode west in search of water. **Raphael Rivera**, an experienced 18-year-old Mexican scout, ventured into the Las Vegas desert. It was there he discovered Las Vegas Springs. Sometime between 1830 and 1848, the name "Vegas," became Las Vegas, Spanish for "the meadows."

The **Mormons** were the first group to settle in the area: In 1855 members of the Church of Latter-Day Saints built a fort out of sun-dried adobe bricks near Las Vegas Creek *(see Historic Sites)*; but it was the advent of the railroad that led to the founding of Las Vegas on May 15, 1905. That was the day that the **Union Pacific** auctioned off 1,200 lots in an area that is now the Fremont Street Experience— a traffic-free, pedestrian mall. In short order, Nevada became the first state to legalize casino-style **gambling**; and then, very reluctantly, the last western state to outlaw it during Prohibition in the first decade of the 20C. At midnight on October 1, 1910, a strict anti-gambling law took effect in Nevada.

Gambling was legalized again in 1931. For many years thereafter, the Mafia ruled Las Vegas. During the early years of The Strip, no holds were barred to attract gamblers—there was no cover

The Strip lights up at night

Bob Brye, Las Vegas News Bureau/LVCVA

charge, no minimum charge, no state speed limit, no sales tax, no waiting period for marriages, no state income tax, and no regulation of gambling, as there is today, however nominal.

In 1966, when billionaire Howard Hughes arrived in the city to live at the Desert Inn (which he purchased), the Nevada legislature finally passed a law allowing publicly traded corporations to obtain gambling licenses. Gradually, legally obtained capital started to flow into the city. Consequently, in the 21C, the financial foundations of Las Vegas are firmly anchored in legitimate corporations, which spare no expense trying to outdo one another to lure gamblers and conventioneers by building one fabulous megaresort after another.

Cashing In On Casinos

By far the most celebrated of the early Las Vegas resorts was the **Flamingo Hotel**, a classy "carpet joint" modeled on the fancy resort hotels in Miami and built by **Benjamin "Bugsy" Siegel**, a member of the Meyer Lansky crime organization. With its giant pink neon sign and replicas of pink flamingos on the lawn, the Flamingo opened on New Year's Eve, 1946. Six months later, Siegel was murdered by an unknown gunman.

CASINOS

Vegas just wouldn't be Vegas without its casinos. The gaming houses that once lit Las Vegas Boulevard with flashing neon have now mushroomed into spectacular themed megaresorts incorporating hotels, restaurants, art museums, animal habitats, and pretty much anything else you can imagine—and some things you can't! Here you'll find reproductions of the Eiffel Tower in Paris, Venice's Grand Canal, and the Sphinx in Egypt. Ogle all you want. If there was ever an eye-popping experience, Vegas is it!

$$$$$ *For a legend of price listings for hotels, see Hotels.*

★★★Bellagio

3600 Las Vegas Blvd. S.
702-693-7111 or 888-987-7111.
www.bellagiolasvegas.com.
3,930 rooms. **$$$$$**

Fine art, gardens, fashion; these are hardly things that you used to associate with a casino in Las Vegas. But that was before this hotel's vision changed the landscape of the gambling mecca. When Steve Wynn opened the $1.7-billion Bellagio in October 1998 (it's now owned by MGM Mirage), he created a place of ideal beauty and comfort. Considered one of the most opulent upscale resorts in the world, this 36-story property was inspired by the village of Bellagio on the shores of Lake Como in northern Italy.

An eight-acre lake, the scene of spectacular **fountain and light shows★★**, graces the front of the complex. Inside, the hotel's casino is arguably the most chic in town; try your hand at a game of Texas Hold 'em or 7-Card Stud in the smoke-free Poker Room or dine with a view at Prime, or Picasso, or even Olives and have the fountains and lake all to yourself. The cavernous 116,000 square foot casino rarely suffers from smoky air. The atmosphere stays clear and scented, perhaps assisted by the spring-like beauty of the lobby with a firmament of glass flowers, each handblown by artist Dale Chihuly. The stunning botanical art abloom in the adjacent conservatory changes its colors and settings with each season.

Bellagio at dusk

★★★The Venetian

3355 Las Vegas Blvd. S.
702-414-4405 or 888-283-6423.
www.venetian.com.
4,047 suites. **$$$$**

Never been to Venice? Don't despair! **St. Mark's Square**, the stately **Doge's Palace**, the **Campanile** and the **Grand Canal**★★ are all closer than you think—at the elegant Venetian in Las Vegas. The world's largest all-suite hotel and convention complex, the Venetian boosted its suite count to a staggering 4,049 units in June 2003 when it opened its Venezia Tower. Designed to painstakingly reproduce the city of Venice, the hotel is located on the site where the venerable Sands Hotel Casino—a Las Vegas institution and the home of the famed Rat Pack—stood from 1952 until it was imploded in 1996. The casino is decked out with reproductions of famous frescoes on the ceilings and marble on the floors. More than 122 table games include a semi-private area for high-stakes Baccarat.

At the Venetian you can update your wardrobe at the **Grand Canal Shoppes** *(see Must Shop)*, which house 75 exclusive retailers, or take a gondola ride—complete with serenade—through the canal that winds around the shops and restaurants and in waters along the frontage along The Strip. Be sure to save up for a dinner at Bouchon or Valentino's *(see Restaurants)*.

The Venetian takes showmanship quite seriously and has added two permanent blockbusters to its nightly roster of stage productions. **Blue Man Group** puts a new spin on its colorful and candid performance each evening and **Phantom of the Opera** was given new life with its own ambient opera house of special effects and a cast that keeps the show sweet and moving within a 90-minute frame, no intermissions.

The Doge's Palace, The Venetian

The Venetian

CASINOS

23

The $1.2-billion property opened in May 1999 with designs on becoming the largest hotel complex in the world and in 2008 it succeeded. The newest addition to The Strip is the **Palazzo Hotel** at the Venetian. It boasts a 50-story luxury tower with approximately 3,025 lavish and large suites, which gives the Venetian the distinction of being the largest hotel in the US (7,025 suites). Find signature dining with such restaurants as CUT by Wolfgang Puck, a sprawling mall of Fifth Avenue-style retail anchored by Barney's New York, and the West Coast home to the "Jersey Boys" straight from Broadway.

If Venetian is the hyperactive young adult, eager to play in a world full of possibility, Palazzo is the impressive and powerful uncle who was to the manner born. Palazzo keeps a refined profile evident immediately in the spacious casino that feels more like an elegant oversized living room than a crowded gaming parlor.

With more than 16 restaurants going hungry is not an option. Although, similar to the adjacent Venetian, Palazzo does not have a buffet. Rather it has names like Lagasse, Trotter and Batali joining Puck in the limelight of culinary splash. In addition there is casual dining at the Grand Lux and Japanese-Brazilian fare at Sushisamba. As the largest hotel campus in the world, the Venetian and Palazzo also share what is probably the largest hotel spa in the world at **Canyon Ranch SpaClub**. Where most hotel spas run around 20,000 square feet and brag if the area sprawls to 30,000, Canyon Ranch SpaClub in Las Vegas counts an improbable 134,000 square feet (think more than two football fields) of sublime pampering. The spa connects the Venetian and the Palazzo around a series of pools and gardens and adds such features as the "Aquavana," a European-inspired suite of thermal cabins, experiential showers, cold rooms and thermal bathing experiences to add to the resort's overall theme of opulence.

★★★Wynn Las Vegas

3131 Las Vegas Blvd. S.
702-770-7000 or 888-320-7123.
www.wynnlasvegas.com.
2,716 rooms. **$$$$$**

No volcanoes, white tigers, wayward pirates or syncopated fountains mark Steve Wynn's latest Las Vegas opus; this curvilinear mocha-colored glass tower is all about class. The "man who made Las Vegas" opened his signature 50-story Strip resort April 28, 2005 on the site of the old Desert Inn. As you enter the hotel from The Strip, you'll find yourself in a blooming, light-filled solarium promenade, teeming with design

---

Sweet!

A stay in the Chairman Suite at Palazzo brings with it four bedrooms, its own pool and garden of Italian statuary, a private putting green and outdoor rainfall shower. Through French doors from the terrace find a baby grand piano by the wet bar and marble fireplace. The marble-laden master spabath comes with infinity tub, sauna, even a salon setup with shampoo sink and barber chair. Your bill for the night? $15,000.

boutiques. Walk down the promenade to see the **Lake of Dreams★★**, where a 140-foot mountain of cascading water dazzles spectators with a multi-media special-effects show twice an hour. Press into the small hall to watch, or enjoy the spectacle while sipping Dom Perignon at the ring-side seats at the two **Parasol lounges**, named for the whimsical parasol light fixtures suspended from their ceilings.

A destination in its own right, the $2.7 billion resort boasts 18 restaurants; a Tom Fazio-designed golf course ($500 per round at peak times); a 2,087-seat theater that stages a water-themed show called Le Rêve; a $40-million, cus-tom-built Broadway Theater that has featured exclusive extended runs of Avenue Q and Spamalot and will soon become the Encore Theater and feature regular appearances by impersonator **Danny Gans** as well as fur-ther shows and headliners. Shoppers and browsers will be duly impressed by the on-site Ferrari-Maserati showroom and souvenir store (you may have to stand in line for a look but you can always jump into the souvenir shop and buy a set of Porsche pencils for $6). You'll also find plenty of designer shopping at the

Wynn Las Vegas

Wynn/Robert Miller

Wynn Esplanade *(see Must Shop)*, where labels like Oscar de la Renta, Manolo Blahnik, Chanel, and Dior abound.

December 2008 brings the open-ing of Wynn's next oeuvre, Encore: an elegant 2,034-suite hotel attached to Wynn and featuring five new restaurants, a smattering of retail, a new ultra nightclub, and a spa all as part of a greater Wynn complex.

★★Caesars Palace

3570 Las Vegas Blvd. S.
702-731-7110 or 800-634-6661.
www.caesars.com.
3,327 rooms. **$$$$**

Chariot of the Goods

- Caesars is the gateway to the $100-million **Forum Shops**, a chi-chi mall cov-ered by a domed ceiling that changes from day to night *(see Must Shop)*. You'll think you're walking down the streets of Rome when you wander amid col-umns, piazzas and statuary.
- Journey into the land Cleopatra would have died for: at **Qua Spa**, you can have a treatment that douses your body in an aromatic massage and then dresses your skin in a design of Swarovski crystals.

CASINOS

The Strip

The city's greatest concentration of resorts and casinos lies along a 4.5-mile stretch of Las Vegas Boulevard known as The Strip. Beginning at the Stratosphere and reaching south to Mandalay Bay *(2000–4000 blocks of Las Vegas Blvd.)*, The Strip is a carnival of sensational architecture and streetside displays. Opening in 2009 is the largest project ever to hit The Strip: The MGM Mirage CityCenter. This $10 billion city within a city is also the world's leading "green project." Measuring 76 acres at mid-Strip, with 6,300 rooms spread across four hotels, 500,000 square feet of retail, dining and entertainment and casino space to match, this marvel also features forward design by leading architects.

Even Julius would have been proud of this majestic hotel that can rightfully claim to be the first theme resort in Vegas. Caesars Palace, which opened in 1966, cost $25 million to build (they've added more than $1 billion in renovations since) and stretches over 85 acres. This Greco-Roman extravaganza encompasses spectacular fountains, three casinos, 12 restaurants, a health spa, a beauty salon, the **Appian Way** shopping area, tennis courts and 4 entertainment lounges. Within its 129,000 square feet of luxe casino space, Caesars offers slot machines that accept denominations of 5¢ to $500. In 1998 Caesars added a 4.5-acre outdoor **Garden of the Gods** with three swimming pools. In 2003 the property experienced a renaissance when the new 4,300-seat **Colosseum** showroom opened, now boasting **Bette Midler**, Cher, Jerry Seinfeld and Elton John as regular headliners. In 2005, the 900-room Augustus Tower and Spa opened and brought with it star restaurants for celebrity chefs Guy Savoy, Bradley Ogden and Bobby Flay. In 2009, Caesars plans to open its newest addition: the 23-story, 665-room **Octavius Tower** as part of a $1 billion expansion that includes three super luxury villas and a trio of lavish pools complementing the Garden of the Gods.

Garden of the Gods, Caesars Palace

NEPTUNES BAR

Caesars Palace

MUST SEE

Sphinx and Pyramid of Luxor Las Vegas

★★Luxor Las Vegas

3900 Las Vegas Blvd. S.
702-262-4000 or 800-288-1000.
www.luxor.com.
4,692 rooms. **$$$**

Imagine ancient Egypt in this 30-story **pyramid**, with a 29-million-cubic-foot atrium at its apex. Fabulous reproductions of artifacts from Luxor, Egypt as well as the Karnak Temple line the walls of the hotel, along with copies of hieroglyphics found in Egypt's Valley of the Kings.

You'll enter the hotel beneath a massive 10-story replica of the

---

Lights in the Kingdom

- By night, a 315,000-watt laser beam—the **Xenon Light★★**—shoots out from the top of the pyramid; it's visible as far as 250 miles away in Los Angeles.

- In the evening hours magician **Criss Angel** comes to life with haunting mindgames of mysticism and illusion; all made stranger by Cirque du Soleil.

- Over in the casino is the world's largest atrium, carved into a cityscape and ancient medina.

Sphinx. From there, you'll be transported to your room by "inclinator," an elevator that travels up the interior slope of the 350-foot pyramid at 39-degrees. But, even the kingdoms of Pharaohs must change and this one is morphing into a vision of what Tut would have wished for in the afterlife.

Luxor has managed to blend hip LA with cool Karnak and the result is a choreographed explosion of new restaurants, shows, nightclubs and attractions bringing this aging pyramid into the 21st century. Find **LAX**, a star-powered nightclub backed by DJ AM and Christina Aguilera, which took over from RA. Aurora is a new lobby lounge full of special effects lighting based on the Aurora Borealis; Company is a 10,000-square-foot restaurant with a fireside lounge surrounded by aspen trees, hurricane lamp candles and a uniquely American menu, all backed by Nicky Hilton, Nick Lachey and Wilmer Valderrama. Noir Bar is a nightclub, tagged as an ultra-exclusive nightspot catering only to the most elite clientele; while Cathouse offers boudoir dining.

That's Entertainment

The MGM Grand has two main showrooms. The first theater was the longtime home of the city's first special-effects spectacle, EFX, which closed in December 2002 and reopened in 2004 as the new home of KÀ, Cirque du Soleil's most dramatic production to date. The second, 700-seat Hollywood Theatre presents star headliners like Craig Ferguson, Lewis Black and David Copperfield, 365 days a year.

MGM Grand

★★MGM Grand

3799 Las Vegas Blvd. South.
702-891-1111 or 800-646-7787.
www.mgmgrand.com.
5,034 rooms. **$$$**

Considered one of the largest hotels in the world, this 114-acre city within a city really roars with amenities: gourmet and specialty restaurants; a 6.6-acre pool and spa complex; Studio 54 nightclub; the 17,157-seat MGM Grand Garden for superstar concerts and world championship sporting events, Studio Walk shopping, and **CBS Television City★**, featuring a studio walk with screening rooms for TV-show pilots.

In 2006 MGM created two new hotels within its grand complex:

Skylofts and Signature. Skylofts is literally a hotel within a hotel for those who want an exclusive Las Vegas experience. Taking up the penthouse floors of the emerald tower, 51 one and two-bedroom suites have the views, the dedicated concierge service, the amenity- and gadget-packed abodes and the privacy.

This comes at a hefty price of course, but this is Vegas at its finest. Aquaphiles will find the six-acre Grand Pool complex alluring. It has five pools, plenty of waterfalls and features, as well as a lazy river running around the rim—all open all year. For scene seekers, daylife can be found at Wet Republic where the barely-in-a-bikini crowd comes to sun and soak.

Lions and Lions and Lions... Oh My!

In MGM Grand's casino, gaming takes on a whole new meaning. Besides 3,500 slot machines and 165 table games, the hotel has real MGM lions right in the middle of the casino. Kids from 8 to 80 will enjoy the **Lion Habitat★**, located near Studio 54 in the middle of the gaming area. Lions romp through the three-story naturalistic structure and walk right over your head (thanks to the wonders of bullet-proof safety glass) in full view. When there are cubs, you can even have a picture taken with them!

Where The Animals Play

The Mirage is home to **The Secret Garden of Siegfried & Roy**★, a lush sanctuary for six rare breeds of exotic cats, including the duo's rare white tigers *(see Animal Acts)*. The habitat provides a way for Siegfried & Roy (conservationists who have established breeding programs on three continents to save the white tiger and white lion from extinction) to share the results of their efforts with the public. Adjoining the Secret Garden is the **Dolphin Habitat**, a breeding and research facility for Atlantic bottlenose dolphins. Guests can meet and frolic with the dolphins up close in a new Trainer for a Day program offered by the hotel.

★★The Mirage

3400 Las Vegas Blvd. S.
702-791-7111 or 800-627-6667.
www.themirage.com.
3,050 rooms. **$$$**

You'll think you're seeing things when you check in at the Mirage—in front of a 20,000-gallon aquarium full of colorful fish (and a few sharks). A few steps into the hotel, you'll find a Polynesian fantasy of lush gardens under a 90-foot-high glass-enclosed atrium filled with royal palms and foliage. The rain-forest theme extends into the casino, where the blackjack tables have the best rules in town. Outside, there's a lagoon with waterfalls and a **volcano**★★ that erupts every 30 minutes after dark with effects and an orchestral score. If this sounds like a tropical paradise, that's what it's supposed to be. This resort, which opened in November 1989 to the tune of $630 million, is credited with being the property that triggered the boom of themed megaresorts up and down the Las Vegas Strip in the early to mid-1990s. Here you can see exotic wildlife in lush habitats, thanks to entertainers Siegfried & Roy, or with **Danny Gans**, enjoy a close encounter of the celebrity kind. **LOVE**, a Beatles-themed Cirque du Soleil production has been packing the house since opening in June 2006.

The Mirage

Las Vegas News Bureau/LVCVA

CASINOS

New York-New York for Sports Fans & Bar Flies

ESPN Zone – A premier sports and dining complex made up of three individual, yet integrated, components. The first is the Studio Grill, where you can enjoy generous portions of American fare. Then there's the Screening Room, featuring two 14-inch screens surrounded by a dozen 36-inch monitors for broadcasting live sports events. Last, but not least, the Sports Arena boasts 10,000 square feet of interactive and competitive games.

Coyote Ugly – This southern-style bar and dance saloon is patterned after the original Coyote Ugly bar in New York City, the one that inspired the blockbuster movie produced by Jerry Bruckheimer. Each night, sexy bartenders climb atop the bar to perform a bold show filled with stunts ranging from fire-blowing to body shots and choreographed dance numbers—and the best part is, you can join in the fun!

★★New York-New York

3790 Las Vegas Blvd. S.
702-740-6969 or 800-693-6763.
www.nynyhotelcasino.com.
2,024 rooms. **$$$**

Start spreading the news: this stellar resort—the tallest casino in Nevada at 47 stories (529 feet)—depicts the familiar New York skyline with re-creations of familiar landmarks. A replica of the **Statue of Liberty★★** is the resort's signature; surrounded by 12 New York City towers, including a version of the **Empire State Building** (47 stories), the Century Building (41 stories) and the Chrysler Building (40 stories). There's even a 300-foot-long model of the **Brooklyn Bridge★**.

The **Manhattan Express**, a Coney Island-style roller coaster, travels around the skyscrapers at speeds of up to 60mph. Around the crowded 84,000sq ft casino, you'll walk by familiar New York sites such as Park Avenue, Central Park, and Times Square.

New York-NewYork is a great place to experience tasty apple martinis; a Coney Island arcade; a bar with dueling pianists; an authentic Irish pub; and Cirque du Soleil's sexiest show ever, *Zumanity*.
See Productions.

New York-New York

Las Vegas News Bureau/LVCVA

★★Paris Las Vegas

3655 Las Vegas Blvd. S.
702-946-7000 or 888-266-5687.
www.parislv.com.
2,916 rooms. **$$$**

Ooh-la-la! If you want to experience the City of Lights and can't afford the air fare, give this hotel a go. Although its namesake city lies across the ocean, Paris Las Vegas strives to capture the essence of Paris, France. Here you can dine 100 feet above The Strip in a 50-story replica of the **Eiffel Tower★★**, or whiz up in a glass elevator to an observation deck overlooking the Las Vegas Valley (not to be confused with the Left Bank).

The place even looks like Paris, with a reproduction of the **Arc de Triomphe**, and façades of **L'Opéra**, the **Louvre** and the **Hôtel de Ville**. The resort opened in September 1999 with Catherine Deneuve, Charles Aznavour and Michel LeGrand in attendance. It cost a cool $790 million to build and its authenticity extends from the French phrases spoken by the employees, to the security guards clad in gendarme uniforms. Three legs of the Eiffel Tower rest on the floor of the casino, whose Parisian streetscapes provide the oh-so-chic setting for 90 table games and more than 1,700 slot machines.

Paris is connected to its sister property, Bally's, by Le Boulevard, a Parisian-style shopping district, complete with cobblestone streets, street lamps and authentic French boutiques and eateries. If you're a pastry lover, don't miss Lenôtre for chocolate and J.J.'s Boulangerie for fresh bread. The

Eiffel Tower
Paris Las Vegas

Paris Las Vegas

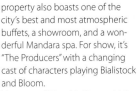

property also boasts one of the city's best and most atmospheric buffets, a showroom, and a wonderful Mandara spa. For show, it's "The Producers" with a changing cast of characters playing Bialistock and Bloom.

Now part of Harrah's Corp., which also owns Caesars, Rio, Bally's, Flamingo and Imperial Palace among others, guests can charge to their room from all Harrah's hotels.

Champagne, Sparkling Wine, Cigars?

A must-not-miss on Le Boulevard at Paris Las Vegas is **Napoleon's Champagne Bar**, which offers a selection of more than 100 champagnes and sparkling wines by the bottle and by the glass, complemented by a light menu of hors d'oeuvres. For smokers, Napoleon's features a cigar bar with a walk-in humidor. Live entertainment nightly makes this a popular night spot.

CASINOS

★★THEhotel at Mandalay Bay

3950 Las Vegas Blvd. S.
702-632-7000 or 877-632-7000.
www.mandalaybay.com.
1,120 rooms. **$$$$**

Although it's attached to Mandalay Bay, this all-suites hotel, opened in December 2003, has its own separate entrance and individual spirit. Beyond the Art Deco lobby you'll find a bar-none spa on the second floor, and Alain Ducasse's acclaimed restaurant, Mix, on the 64th floor—accessible by its own glass elevator. There's also a sky lounge with a terrace for lingering over the lights of the city. The average suite measures 750 square feet and comes with three plasma televisions, high-speed internet, a deep soaking tub, and a wonderfully comfy bed.

Mandalay Bay links to Luxor through the **Mandalay Place** shopping complex *(see Must Shop)*, located along a 310-foot-long sky bridge.

★★Treasure Island Las Vegas

3300 Las Vegas Blvd. S. at
Spring Mountain Rd.
702-894-7111 or 800-288-7206.
www.treasureislandlasvegas.com.
2,900 rooms. **$$$**

When Steve Wynn first opened this hotel in 1993, the drawbridge from The Strip led to the world of Robert Louis Stevenson's 1883 adventure novel *Treasure Island*. Outside, waves lapped at a replica of a small island village. Inside, overflowing treasure chests lined the walls, carpets were patterned with jewels and gold doubloons,

Treasure Island

and stolen treasure hung above the casino tables.

The booty is now gone from the rafters—and so is the name. Treasure Island was rebranded as TI in 2004 and the famed Pirate's Battle in front of the hotel was traded for a steamy song-and-dance show performed by sexy girls—billed as the **Sirens of TI**—in wet, skin-tight rags. The ancient Mediterranean fishing village frontage is still there, although it's now used as nightclub and dining terraces.

The Bathhouse

3950 Las Vegas Blvd. S. 702-632-7000 or 877-632-7000. www.the hotelatmandalaybay.com.

The $25-million, 14,000-square-foot spa **Bathhouse** spa has been receiving attention for its austere design, incorporating ultrasuede-lined walls, charcoal-colored slate, cool glass, and lots of falling water within its textured geometric spaces. The two-story complex contains hot and cold plunge pools, eucalyptus steam rooms, redwood saunas, and dimly lit relaxation rooms.

REST OF THE BEST: MORE CASINOS

Las Vegas never sleeps—and that goes for the cranes and backhoes at work 24/7 building new and ever more fantastic structures to fuel the appetites and shake the wallets of anyone in need of a quick break. At least a dozen hotels are online to go up by 2012, all with new casinos, restaurants and attractions that will make your head swirl.

★Planet Hollywood

3667 Las Vegas Blvd. S.
702-791-7827 or 877-333-WISH.
www.planethollywood.com.
2,600 rooms. **$$$**

The 1001 Nights of Aladdin has morphed into the Swarovski crystal lights of Planet Hollywood, officially opened in September 2007 with a glamor-laden lobby, clean edged casino floor and suites that play upon the lives of celebrities, each with its own mini-museum of memorabilia. LA is everywhere here, from Pink's Hot Dogs in the Race and Sports Book Lounge to KOI Restaurant, straight from La Cienega Blvd. to the Miracle Mile fashion mall that circles the property with 170 upscale chain stores and boutiques, dining venues such as 🍴**Trader Vic's** and a smattering of nightclubs.

The casino is a large and roomy venue that has the Heart Bar at its center, a slick and clean-edged venue where a martini feels right. The casino also puts a novel Las Vegas stamp on gaming with the Pleasure Pit. From 8pm until the midnight hours the game is on and so is the dance, as go-go girls in scanty hot-wear rock it out on pedestals above the gaming tables. Dealers, too, put on their teddies and bustiers for the evening as the casino bets on players losing their shirts.

Those who want to dance get their chance at 🍴**Privé**, an ultralounge scene where shot girls in hotpants offer drinks on the dance floor, while guests at the VIP tables get doting service with their $500 bottles of champagne.

★Circus Circus

2880 Las Vegas Blvd. S.
702-734-0410 or 800-634-3450.
www.circuscircus.com.
4,000 rooms. **$**

Opened in 1968, Circus Circus was the city's first gaming establishment to offer entertainment for all ages. Initially there was a casino and a carnival midway, but no hotel rooms. The first 400 rooms were built in 1972. Today the casino occupies the main floor, while the second floor is a fantasy of carnival games, state-of-the-art arcade games and a 🍴**circus arena**. 🍴The **Adventuredome** indoor theme park was added in 1993 (*see Musts for Kids*).

Today, the show must go on and the daily roster of circus acts that made this property famous continue with an impressive array of talent that comes from all over the world to make it in Las Vegas. It is possible to pull slots and hit your soft 12 while trapeze artists fly above you. For those who want in on the game, Circus Circus is one of the few casinos in town that offer free gaming lessons at set times each day. Hungry guests should check the buffet—still one of the best deals in town.

Excalibur

Excalibur Hotel & Casino

★Excalibur

3850 Las Vegas Blvd. S.
702-597-7777 or 800-937-7777.
www.excalibur-casino.com.
4,008 rooms. **$$**

Ever dream of traveling back in time to an age of jousting knights? Enter the world of King Arthur (a great place to bring the kids) via this sparkling medieval castle. In **King Arthur's Arena** you can eat with your hands and cheer the action during the Tournament of Kings. Keeping with the Camelot theme, the hotel's shopping mall is a medieval village. There's also a male dance revue that would likely make King Arthur blush. Excalibur remains friendly to families, despite some growing up it has done recently. Following a bottom to top redo of the rooms, the property recently completed a redesign of the pool area, with four pools, brand spanking new cabanas, fire pits, sun decks and a secluded relaxation pool. There are ten cabanas designed especially for those traveling with children. Hungry swimmers can have food delivered via the new poolside restaurant, Drenched. Cabana rentals start at $125.

Reconstruction of the new pool and cabanas at Excalibur

Excalibur Hotel & Casino

★Mandalay Bay Resort & Casino

3950 Las Vegas Blvd. S.
702-632-7777 or 877-632-7000.
www.mandalaybay.com.
3,660 rooms. **$$**

Life is a beach at Mandalay Bay. This tropical-themed resort possesses the only sand-and-surf beach on The Strip. Besides its casino, the property boasts an 11-acre **lagoon**, a three-quarter-mile lazy river ride, 15 restaurants, nightclubs, shops, **Shark Reef★★** aquarium *(see Animal Acts)*, and the renowned House of Blues (don't miss their Sunday Gospel brunch). You can take a monorail from Mandalay Bay to its sister properties, Luxor and Excalibur. Rooms here are large and luxurious and offer fabulous views of The Strip. Summer turns the resort into ground zero for scene-style fun with one of The Strip's few European bathing pools and summer rock concerts that can be experienced from the beach pool.

★The Palms Casino Resort

4321 W. Flamingo Rd.
702-942-7064 or 866-725-6773.
www.palms.com.
1,003 rooms. **$$$**

Built in 2001, this 55-story tower just off The Strip appeals to those who know the casino offers video-poker machines with some of the best odds in the city. At night, The Palms comes alive with pool parties at Skin, and late-night action at **Rain Nightclub** and **Ghost Bar** *(see Nightlife)*. The beds are famous, for comfort and size; "NBA rooms" accommodate

The Palms Casino & Resort

Bowling alley in the Palms KingPin Fantasy Suite

the tallest of guests. In 2006 Palms opened the 40-story Fantasy Tower with a series of suites geared to grab your attention. How about a suite with a bowling alley, or one with a full complement of basketball courts? If it can be dreamed up, the Palms will have it.

Stratosphere

2000 Las Vegas Blvd. S.
702-380-7777 or 800-998-6937.
www.stratlv.com.
2,444 rooms. **$$**

This property is the height of Vegas spectacular—its 1,149-foot **tower★** is the tallest freestanding structure west of the Mississippi. Test your fate on **Insanity** and be dangled over the edge of the tower, ride the **Big Shot** to be shot up it's spire, or take the X-Scream to teeter-totter above the clouds. In addition, there's a revolving restaurant in the needle, and two observation decks with great **views★★★**, so you can literally keep your nose in the air for hours. Check out American Superstars, Las Vegas' longest running afternoon production, or cool off at the roof pool on the 8th floor.

Flamingo Las Vegas

3555 Las Vegas Blvd. S.
702-733-3111 or 800-732-2111.
www.flamingolasvegas.com.
3,642 rooms. **$$-$$$**

The name Flamingo Hotel has survived from the 1940s era of Strip development, but in 1993 the Hilton Corporation razed the Flamingo's original motel-style buildings (created by gangster Bugsy Siegel), with its false stairways and bulletproof office. Today, the Flamingo comprises six towers of guest rooms, a wedding chapel, and a wildlife habitat. A top to bottom redo in 2006 and 2007 brought the "GO" room to the Flamingo, an Austin Power's-like pad of bubble gum pinks, sandy beiges and whites with bedside controls that move the drapes open and shut and lots of shiny plastic furniture details to put it all together. The pool is one of the lushest on The Strip, with waterfalls, wildlife and greenery.

Flamingo Las Vegas

Flamingo Las Vegas

Tropicana Resort & Casino

3801 Las Vegas Blvd. S.
702-739-2222 or 800-634-4000.
www.tropicanalv.com.
1,800 rooms. **$$-$$$**

In recent years, this Polynesian-themed hotel has undergone renovations that include the creation of a shopping arcade. Splash around in the water park, equipped with three pools (featuring swim-up blackjack in summer), five spas, two tropical lagoons, and live flamingos. Noted for the 4,000-square-foot **stained-glass ceiling** that curves over the casino floor, The Tropicana also hosts the popular **Folies Bergere** *(see Productions).*

Rio Suites

3700 W. Flamingo Rd.
702-777-7777 or 888-746-7482.
www.playrio.com.
2,554 rooms. **$$**

Rio started the "suite" trend when it opened in 1990. Each "suite" is actually an oversized room with a large sofa area that can be used for sleeping. But the company got the jump on attractions when it opened its Masquerade in the Sky show over the casino area, which is a wonderfully creative mélange of New Orleans-style costumes and props with electric dancing and music. Sky floats allow guests to ride with the action once an hour above the casino floor. The hotel also offers a happening party daily at the Sapphire pool (admission charged), and an adults only scene at Lucky Strike Lanes bowling.

Red Rock Resort

1101 W. Charleston Blvd.
702-797-7777 or 866-767-7773.
www.redrocklasvegas.com.
460 rooms. **$$-$$$**

This resort marks the flagship for Station Casinos, a locals' fave known for great values on dining and rooms and gaming odds. But this property brings the offerings to a new and quality level of hipness, handsome décor, spacious and comfortable rooms and action-packed scenes. Crystal and rock is the theme here—and rock extends to outdoor concerts in the pool. A fabulous spa integrates the nearby desert into its programs.

Golden Nugget

129 E. Fremont St.
702-385-7111 or 800-634-3454.
www.goldennugget.com.
1907 rooms. **$$**

Downtown Las Vegas might just be the city's best-kept secret for fun and value; a stay at the Golden Nugget underscores this point. Suites here are huge and rent for the price of a small Strip

hotel room. After a top to bottom $100 million redo in 2006 it has a cabana-lined pool with a three-story shark tank in the middle (and a see-through slide that tunnels right through it), new restaurants, a happening nightclub, a redone casino, and Downtown's only spa. For a modest fee you can have VIP check-in and concierge service.

South Point Hotel

9777 Las Vegas Blvd S.
702-796-7111 or 866-796-7111.
2163 rooms. **$$**

Located on the Southern end of The Strip, South Point is ground zero for activities and events during the National Finals Rodeo week and keeps that spirit kindled with clubs and acts that appeal to the Western spirit. It has a huge equestrian center as well as a bowling alley, kids club, cinema-plex, bingo hall, spa, salon, barber, fitness center—a place you never need to leave, although some of the city's best shopping is a stone's throw away. Rooms are oversized, relatively new (Dec 2005) and all is reasonably priced here.

Lobby, Red Rock Resort

GAMBLING

Oh, the games people play—blackjack, craps, keno, roulette, slot machines, and more. Gambling made the city what it is, and gambling remains its tour de force. Here are a few of the games of chance that gambling brings to the table (don't forget to tip your dealer):

Blackjack – The object is to draw cards that add up to 21 or as close to 21 as possible without going over that magic number. Everybody at the table bets against the dealer. If the dealer's first two cards total 16 or under, the dealer must "hit," or draw additional cards. If they add up to 17 or over, the dealer must stand. If the player's cards add up to more than the dealer's, but are under 21, the player wins. If the situation is reversed, the house wins (or they can tie and nobody wins).
An ace and a face card or a ten together constitute blackjack, which automatically wins (except in the case of a tie).

Craps – On the first or "come out" roll in this fast-paced dice game, the "shooter" throws the dice to the other end of the table (dice must hit the wall of the table to be considered a legal roll). The shooter tries to establish a number—four, five, six, eight, nine or ten—then he tries to roll that number again before he rolls a seven.

Roulette – The roulette table is covered with 36 numbers plus a green zero and a green double zero (the European layout has only one zero). Half of the 36 numbers are red and half are black. Players may place chips on any combination of numbers. The winner is determined by where the marble-like ball comes to rest when the croupier spins the wheel. Players can wager on black or red, even or odd, high or low, and even zero or double zero to enhance or complement their numbers or to get even odds on a spin. They can even put money on the corner or line of a number and split the risk among two or four numbers. But if a single number comes in with a wager squarely upon it, the pay out is 36 to one. Sweet!

Slots – These machines are as much about entertainment as they are about the jackpot. Nickel slots can still be found in most casinos. Quarters are more the standard, although you can play $1 to $500 in coin or token. Many machines taken on cartoon or movie themes and have an animated production that takes over for a bonus game

Who's Your Daddy?

If slots or video poker is your game, sign up for the player's club; all casinos have them. These memberships allow you to accrue points as you play. The casino will reward your business with free restaurant vouchers, free play coupons, and maybe even a room. You'll get the house logo trucker's cap just for signing, and if you play enough, you'll be invited back—on the house.

if you make a certain combo in the roll. Players are advised to play all the lines—which usually means dropping nine or more coins for the maximum bet in each roll in order to keep the odds in their favor. To make the slots really pay off, join a players club. Then, simply insert the points card into the machine and watch the points add up with each play, win or lose. Points accrue quickly and come in handy for free buffet meals or dinners at the house gourmet room.

Baccarat – Baccarat calls for a tux and a 'tini, shaken—not stirred. Its considered a high-class card game because of high minimum bets waged in gold-plated rooms beneath glistening crystal. But even if it was the preferred game for Bond, it's dynamics are simple. Plus it offers some of the lowest house edges in the joint, allowing you to retrieve 99% of what you wager if you can hold out long enough. As with blackjack, two hands are dealt, and the higher hand wins. You can bet on either hand to win: the "Banker" or the "Player." Betting on the "Player" has a house edge of 1.24%, and betting on "Banker" has an edge of 1.06%. Even with the 5% commission added to a "Banker" win, it is still the best Baccarat play. Each player gets a turn to deal. Preset rules dictate whether a given hand can pull a third card, but three cards is the max, no matter what. The hand closer to nine wins. And unlike Blackjack, there's no such thing as a bust in Baccarat. Only the last digit of a two-card total over nine is counted (Ace is one, face is zero). Try to play at a crowded table for

the best chance of holding on to your bankroll.

Video Poker – Slot lovers should take the video poker challenge for the best return for their time and money. It requires strategy and offers a decent chance to win good payoffs. The five coin max bet is recommended. The machine deals five cards, which can be kept or tossed by tapping the screen. Then you hit the DRAW button and you get replacement cards for the cards not kept. You win if you wind up with a poker hand of two pair, straight, flush, etc. Payouts depend on the style of machine played, and on its paytable, usually explained on top of the machine. Always wager the maximum as a sizable bonus reward is paid for a royal flush.

Video poker offers some of the best odds in the casino, if a player plays well. Certain video poker machines have a return of over 100% with proper play, especially Deuces Wild, which pays up to 100.77%. You can find these machines downtown and in locals' casinos rather than The Strip.

Las Vegas News Bureau/LVCVA

The Tropicana's stained-glass ceiling

VEGAS HEADLINERS

Frank Sinatra, Jerry Lewis, Dean Martin and Sammy Davis Jr. were among the names that took Vegas from a two-horse town to the entertainment capital of the world. When a star feels like playing it big, it means a Vegas tour, as Streisand did for her final official concerts, as Diana Ross did for her famous shows at Caesars, and as legends like Tony Bennett, Tom Jones and Elton John continue to do today. Although the headliner is steadily disappearing to an onslaught of production shows and the prolific creativity of Cirque du Soleil, there are still a few of these marquees blazing above the Vegas Strip. One of these is now Bette Midler.

🎤 Bette Midler

At Caesars Palace Colosseum,
3570 Las Vegas Blvd. S.
702-731-7110 or 877-423-5463.
bette.aeglive.com.
Dark Thursdays and Sundays.

Although she admits to being intimidated by the 4,100-seat theater (the $95 million Colosseum stage is one of the largest in the world), the 61-year-old Divine Miss M is no stranger to the big stage. Midler made her Broadway debut in the original "Fiddler on the Roof" and went on to win a Tony Award for her work in 1974, Oscar nominations for her performances in "For the Boys" and "The Rose," and a Grammy for "Wind Beneath My Wings" as the 1989 Record of the Year.

She has played to sold-out arenas in Las Vegas during the city's pricy New Year's celebrations and has now agreed to take on Caesars Palace, playing 100 nights a year in a two-year contract counting down from February 20, 2008. The deal has her singing for one show, five nights for 20 weeks this year—and playing exclusively at Caesars during those weeks. Elton John takes up some of the balance with his Red Piano concert engagements. Heavyweight headliners Cher and Jerry Seinfeld also put in time at the Colosseum.

No doubt Midler's 90-minute show is seen as a display of her usual style of outrageous, flamboyant, over-the-top energy, full of '40s-style Sophie Tucker nods that likely go over the heads of many of today's youth.

The timelessness of her work: "Do You Wanna Dance," "From a Distance," even "Bugle Boy," however, close any gap in question. Then there is the memorable tear-grabber, "One for My Baby,"

Bette Midler

Caesars Palace

Great White Way West

Broadway has finally come to Las Vegas with such Tony-winning hits as *Jersey Boys* at Palazzo, **Phantom of the Opera** at The Venetian, and *The Producers* at Paris Las Vegas. Meanwhile, Cirque du Soleil opened **LOVE** at the Mirage, *KÁ* at MGM Grand, and the sexy *Zumanity* at New York-New York. In its latest production, *Believe*—a show featuring Mindfreak's **Criss Angel** (opened at Luxor in September 2008)—the troupe reinvents the traditional magic show in a custom-designed theater that fuses Angel's revolutionary illusions and mind-blowing artistry with acrobatics, dance, puppetry, music and poetry for a bizarre and fascinating journey to the edges of entertainment. It will be followed by an Elvis-themed production in 2009 at CityCenter. To keep audiences piqued and playing, most shows in Las Vegas run 90 minutes.

which closed that Carson Show for the last time.

Midler intersperses her power-numbers with familiar nods to the odd entertainment characters that have dominated showbiz in Las Vegas over the years. One Delores DeLago, a wheelchair-bound lounge diva seems quite at home, singing a round of Elvis Presley and Frank Sinatra hits. Then there is Soph, the Sophie Tucker-style bawdy jokestress remade into a saucy showgirl.

Rather than capitalize on the high-tech hydraulics of the stage, Ms. M fills the stage with her own big talent and a line-up of glittery showgirls.

Connecting with her audience is Midler's great art and she gives it her all with voice, humor and occasional pop-in visits from former partner and friend Barry Manilow, who is performing down the street. Tickets are $95 to $250.

Barry Manilow: Music and Passion

At the Las Vegas Hilton,
3000 Paradise Rd.
702-739-2222 or 800-222-5361.
www.lv-hilton.com.

Barry Manilow spent a good chunk of his time telling fans that if they wanted to see him perform, they would have to come to his house. Happily for his fans, Manilow now has a new home at the 1,700-seat Hilton Theater in the Las Vegas Hilton where he performs *Manilow:*

Barry Manilow

Barry, Bette Midler's former pianist and musical director, admits that his strength lies in musical arrangements; "I'm a fair singer, I write nice songs, but I'm a great arranger.

My songs are like anchovies. Some people love them—some people get nauseous." So far, he has sold about 60 million records.

Rita Rudner

At Harrah's Las Vegas,
3475 Las Vegas Blvd. S.,
702-369-5222 or 800-214-9110.
www.ritafunny.com.

Harrah's Entertainment Las Vegas

Rita Rudner

Music and Passion Wednesday through Saturday.

His extended contract runs through 2009 so far, and the singer, who has rounded 60, shows no signs of slowing down. After more than three decades of performing and a career that has produced more than 50 albums, Manilow performs five shows a week, dutifully dusting off such hits as "Mandy," "It's a Miracle," "Could It Be Magic?" "I Write the Songs," and "Copacabana." He also throws in some pop numbers mixing high-tech sounds with the Las Vegas classics once performed by Frank Sinatra, Elvis Presley, Sammy Davis Jr., and Dean Martin.

To most people, doing an almost nightly live stage show, having your own daily television show, writing a book, and being a wife and mother all at the same time would be enough to make you bonkers.

Comedienne Rita Rudner, who performs regularly at Harrah's most nights of the week, is doing it all. Wife to writer/producer Martin Bergman and mother to adopted daughter, Molly, and pet canine (aptly named Bonkers after her grandfather), Rita works like a dog during each of her stage shows, as she unleashes her talents on a waiting world.

Packing A Punch Line

While Rudner admits that it's never easy to come up with new material, she tries every night to introduce one new thought. If she's lucky, she'll get one or two jokes a week that she's very proud to weave into her act. Rudner writes all her own material, focusing on relationship humor and common experiences, jotting her thoughts down in notebooks that she reviews a half-hour before the show. Always on the lookout for new ideas, Rudner says that when someone pulls on a door that says "Push," she knows there's material for comedy there—after all, she's done it herself a million times.

MUST SEE

The Scintas

The Scintas

At the Las Vegas Hilton
3000 Paradise Rd.,
702-739-2222 or 800-222-5361.
www.thescintas.com.

The Hilton serves up sibling revelry six nights a week. That's Scinta (pronounced *SHIN-tah*) as in Joe, Frank, and Christine (Chrissi) Scinta, along with adopted cohort Peter O'Donnell. During the evening, you may hear tales of other relatives—Grandpop Kunta Scinta, Uncle Fulla Scinta, and Aunt Stepina Pila Scinta—the Scintas keep things in the family.
Of course, it's hard to know what to expect from an act that was categorized by one entertainment critic as a cross between the Village People, Don Rickles and Cher. One thing's for certain—no one is exempt from being picked on. At the end of the night, though, you'll leave reassured that the Scinta family loves their audiences as much as they love performing. All who have seen the act agree that it's not just their tremendously talented combination of music, comedy and impressions

(complete with wigs and props) that has put the group at the hub of Las Vegas. It's also their habit of tugging at the heartstrings of their audiences with their obvious family devotion, stories and songs. The Scintas have never been scripted; they simply go out on stage and have fun in their own unique way. If you have any doubt, the production number in the beginning of the show reflects the true image of who they are: family.

The Family Business

To sum up the Scintas' 90-minute act in a few words, Joe is on bass and does a right-on Mick Jagger as well as playing comedic foil to younger brother Frank.
Self-taught musician Frank plays virtually every instrument, does a range of impressions that brings down the house, then takes on Peter O'Donnell (the only non-Sicilian Scinta) for the ultimate comedic percussion duet. Enter younger sister Chrissi, who lights up the stage with her powerful soprano voice.

PRODUCTIONS
QUINTESSENTIAL VEGAS

One of the attributes of Las Vegas that puts a feather in the city's cap was the Las Vegas showgirl. With her plumed headdresses and long legs, she and the lavish productions in which she appeared became synonymous with the city in its early years. Alas, the day of the Vegas showgirl is gone, replaced by flashier productions that appeal to a more sophisticated audience with higher-tech tastes in risqué productions. Still, if you hanker for good old-fashioned entertainment, these two Vegas classics are a good bet.

✥ Folies Bergere

At the Tropicana,
3801 Las Vegas Blvd. S.
702-739-2411 or 800-829-9034.
www.tropicanalasvegas.com.
(Shows at 8:30pm and 10pm
are topless).

Legs, legs, and more legs. Modern audiences have Lou Walters, former entertainment director of the Tropicana (father of TV news correspondent Barbara Walters), to thank for introducing Americans to a theatrical form that has been around since 1866. Today the Folies Bergere is the longest continually running show in the US. In 1975 when the Folies Bergere moved from its 16 year home at the Tropicana's Fountain Theatre into the new 950-seat Tiffany Theatre, it truly became an American

The First Folies

Paris' first music hall, the glamorous Folies Bergère Theatre, opened in 1869 on the grounds of a 13C monastery. The first nude showgirl appeared on the Folies stage in 1918, changing the show's reputation forever. In the 1920s the Folies began to evolve into a large-scale production. The show reached its pinnacle in the 1930s and '40s, however, when stars such as singer Josephine Baker took the stage.

institution (as well as an original production). Every new edition of the show since then has been unique, with new costuming, new production numbers, original choreography and elaborate new sets (the show maintains the historical "Folies" name and is licensed by special arrangement with the original Folies Bergère in Paris.) The latest edition of the Folies Bergere is a contemporary salute to beautiful women through the years, from 1850 to the present. Of course, the show retains the award-winning Can-Can number, which has been an integral part of the production since 1975.

Tropicana/Kirvin Doak Communications: Francis Bayton

Donn Arden's Jubilee!

*At Bally's Las Vegas,
3645 Las Vegas Blvd S.
800-237-7469. www.ballyslv.com.
Late show (10:30pm) is topless.*

It may have modern-day costumes, sets, sound, lights, choreography and a nearly 100-member cast, but Jubilee! is still a throwback to Las Vegas' Golden Age of lavish stage spectaculars. Having celebrated its 25th anniversary in 2006, **Jubilee!** is the second-longest running show on The Strip (after Folies Bergere). The quintessential Vegas-style revue was conceived by the late Donn Arden, best known for introducing the Lido de Paris—and the topless showgirl—to the city in the mid-1950s.

When it premiered in 1981 at what was then the MGM Grand, Jubilee! was bigger and more spectacular than any other show on The Strip, and far more expensive. The original staging of Jubilee! cost $10 million. Lead character Delilah's jeweled headpiece alone originally cost $3,000 and contained 20lbs of rhinestones. More than 1,000 costumes are worn during the

Fun Facts

A hundred different sets require some 100,000 light bulbs and over 125 miles of wiring; 4,200lbs of dry ice are used each week; 10lbs of explosives burst nightly in 50 pyrotechnic effects; during the iceberg scene in the "Titanic" number, 5,000 gallons of recycled water cascade across the stage; 8,000 miles of sequins, two tons of feathers and 10,000 pounds of jewelry are used; the heaviest feathered headdress weighs 35lbs —the heaviest hat? 20lbs.

show, many of them designed by world-renowned designers Bob Mackie and Pete Menefee.

Based on Jerry Herman's Hundreds of Girls, the opening act features 76 performers in feathered headdresses. In the Ziegfeld Follies-style ending, the entire cast, dressed in jaw-dropping garb, walks down a 50-step staircase to the tune of "A Pretty Girl Is Like a Melody"— a Vegas classic. The show ends with a bang as the stage turns into the Titanic, which sinks in a frenzy of leggy action.

Showgirls, Donn Arden's Jubilee!

Bally's Las Vegas

CIRQUE DU SOLEIL

This extraordinary troupe started as a group of street performers in Baie-Saint-Paul, Quebec, in 1982. The company now has almost 4,000 employees from over 40 different countries, including more than a 1,000 artists. Cirque du Soleil currently has six shows in Vegas… and counting. Cirque is also the creative influence behind the 🎭**Revolution Lounge** at the Mirage, its first foray into spheres beyond pure performance. However, the circus is always its center stage, and to keep its productions stocked with the world's top triple jointed talents, Las Vegas has a circus school, one of the few in the US. On any given day one can find Cirque performers and Cirque hopefuls dangling and dancing on lines of silk from a 50-foot ceiling, or balancing on a rope closer to the ground. Injuries on stage are not uncommon. Once in the Cirque, it is a life-long commitment, whether as a performer finding impossible ways to move muscles, or as a teacher.

🎭Mystère

At Treasure Island,
3300 Las Vegas Blvd. S. ; 800-392-1999. www.treasureisland.com.

Hoping to find real treasure at Treasure Island? It comes in the form of performance without boundaries, ballet without gravity and theater without actors. It's Mystère: a surrealistic celebration of music, dance, acrobatics and comedy from the artistic body that holds the patent on imagination-bending—Cirque du Soleil. Although the 72-odd member cast incorporates basic circus concepts in their productions, any similarity to any circus you have ever seen before ends there. Relying on the performers and their limitless creativity, Mystère presents stunning feats on the trapeze, Korean plank, and Chinese poles, as well as an aerial bungee ballet.

"O"

At Bellagio,
3600 Las Vegas Blvd. S.
888-488-7111; 702-693-7722.
www.bellagio.com.

The star of this Cirque du Soleil spectacle (at Bellagio for an indefinite run) is 1.5 million gallons of water, representing the circle of life. With this mesmerizing show, the troupe ventures for the first time into aquatic theater, wherein Cirque du Soleil reaches fascinating new heights. From the moment the curtain parts to reveal a forest-like setting on stage, the mysteries of "O" begin to unfold. Floors disappear into pools of water and walls vanish in the mist. The cast of 74 synchronized swimmers, divers, contortionists and trapeze artists perform incredible feats in and over this liquid stage, which transforms itself from one body of water to another in the space of a few seconds.

KÀ

At MGM Grand,
3799 Las Vegas Blvd. S.
702-891-1111 or 877-264-1845.
www.ka.com.

Just when you thought Cirque du Soleil could not possibly dream up another amazing theater-of-the-bizarre production, along comes KÀ, which may well be their best endeavor to date. Named after an Egyptian word for the invisible spirit duplicate of the body that accompanies each person throughout this life and into the next, KÀ blends fire and special effects with riveting results. Eighty athletic performers infuse martial arts, acrobatics, puppetry, interactive video and pyrotechnics to support a plot that spotlights imperial twins (a boy and girl) who take off on a danger-laden adventure that separates their fates and ultimately reunites them.

The tale moves through 27 haunting sequences of purifying and destructive fire, dreamscapes of storms and floods, tender moments of shadow puppetry, and precipitous battle scenes staged on an impossibly tilted stage, which at one point, rotates—with the performers on it—a full 360 degrees. Humorous encounters with gigantic sand-dwelling crustaceans add to the fun. The Cirque's signature bungee props and swing poles are featured in ethereal numbers, all enhanced by an extraordinary score of chorus and orchestra.

Mystère

Cirque du Soleil

Love

At Mirage,
3400 Las Vegas Blvd. S.
702-791-7111 or 800-963-9634.
www.thebeatleslove.com.

The Cirque opened the Beatles-themed production inside a 360-degree custom-created theater at the Mirage in 2006 using the master tapes at Abbey Road Studios to create a multi-sensory Beatles experience that is as dazzling to watch as it is to hear. Employing film projections of the Fab Four as a backdrop against a dazzling continuum of impossible choreography, mesmerizing special effects, and riveting costume and inventive stage design, the show marks the fist time in the Cirque's two dozen years that actual lyrics are integral to the music. The show and music is everywhere through, at some counts, 6,000 speakers including those built into each and every seat. "Love" was all that was needed to fulfil an aspiration inspired by the friendship between George Harrison and Cirque director Gilles Ste-Croix. The results are stunning. You've never heard the Beatles like this.

Zumanity

At New York-New York,
3970 Las Vegas Blvd. S.
702-740-6969.
www.zumanity.com.

Nudity is just another costume in this sexy Cirque du Soleil show where acrobatics, languid ballet moves, and amazing feats of human physicality produce one wow after another. It's performed in the style of European cabaret theater in acts with names like "2Men" and "Gentle Orgy"—get the picture?

47

VEGAS FAVORITES

Nowhere is Las Vegas'"wow" factor more apparent than in its production shows. Here are a few of our favorites.

Stomp Out Loud

At Planet Hollywood,
3667 Las Vegas Blvd.
702-785-5000 or 877-333-9474.
www.stompoutloudvegas.com.

Planet Hollywood Resort opened to plenty of fanfare—and Barbra Streisand fans—when it finally did its grand opening thing in late 2007. But the resort that rose from the relics of the legendary Aladdin started rocking long before diamonds and divas came out for the party. Stomp Out Loud opened on April 17, 2007, to celebrate percussion in its perfection in a 1,500-seat signature theater built just for this show.

You won't hear dialog—spoken dialog—in the show. Rather all communication is done through sound and beats in a line-up of numbers that build to a simply wild entertainment experience. There are a total of 24 performers in the Stomp Out Loud company. Twelve cast members are Stomp veterans and 12 are new to the Las Vegas Company. Sixteen Stompers perform in each show. The show's directors played drums in new wave punk bands in London and started working together as part of a street band in 1981. After becoming a regular part of Britain's alternative comedy and music scene, they began to experiment with found percussion concepts that eventually became Stomp.

The audience is invited to create some percussive moments of their own in the show lobby, where a labyrinth of odd metal objects invites playful exploration.

Found Sound

A major element in the show is water, which falls at 3.5 gallons per minute on each performer in "Rain." Another number, "Waterphonics," uses two tanks with 539 gallons of water. For drier numbers, 18 garbage cans and 24 lids are used, all imported from the UK especially for this production.

Stomp Out Loud

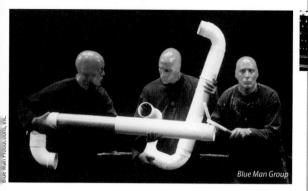

Blue Man Group

🎭 Blue Man Group

At The Venetian,
3355 Las Vegas Blvd. S.
702-414-1000 or 888-283-6423.
www.blueman.com.

If you haven't seen Blue Man Group, by all means, do. In 2005 the unique blue-hued trio moved from Luxor, where the show had been playing since March 2000, to a 1,750-seat theater built just for them at the Venetian. Surprises galore await audiences already mesmerized by drum beats and syncopated colors enhanced by tubes, shadows and effects. The show can be seen again and again as no two are the same.

🎭 La Femme

At MGM Grand,
3799 Las Vegas Blvd. S.
702-891-7777.
www.mgmgrand.com.

Straight from the Crazy Horse in Paris, this intimate feminine revue celebrates women in a way that Americans rarely do. The stage fills with 13 dancers, chosen for their lithe bodies, flexibility and ability

to turn on the energy with just a smile. Spare costuming gives way to elaborate stage props and engaging musical performances on the small stage.

All seats here are good ones and put the audience right up to the action—a rare experience in a town where most performances are watched from a distance. Spots for the troupe here are very competitive. Dancers often hail from Russian ballet academies and lives of strict classical training.

La Femme

PRODUCTIONS

49

Le Rêve

Le Rêve

Wynn Las Vegas,
3131 Las Vegas Blvd.
702-770-9966 or 888-320-7110.
www.wynnlasvegas.com.

Opened in 2005, Le Rêve (French for "the dream") plays in the Wynn Theatre, a 2,087-seat theater in the round. The show immerses 75 Cirque-du-Soleil-trained artists into a watery stage for 90 minutes of glorious dream sequences. This work is the achievement of Franco Dragone, former director of Cirque du Soleil. As in a dream, the haunting sequences meld together and

the message is what you make it. If you sit in the first three rows of any section, prepare to get soaked (the staff passes out towels before the show).

Phantom of the Opera

At The Venetian,
3355 Las Vegas Blvd.
702-414-9000 or 877-883-6423.
www.phantomlasvegas.com.

Phantom never seems to go out of style. See it once, see it two dozen times, it still delights the soul and rivets the imagination no matter how many times you have seen the chandelier drop. See it in Vegas, however, and see it anew. First, the show has been fine-tuned for the standard 90-minute Vegas format. Second, the show plays in a custom-built theater designed with the greatest of care to give the illusion that you are actually in the Paris Opera House. Third, the staging employs a variety of impressive special effects and fourth—audiences have the rare, if not exceptional, opportunity to take a stage tour and go backstage to meet the cast—including the Phantom, unmasked.

Le Rêve

AFTERNOON SHOWS

Las Vegas has always been looked upon as a late-night town. But the fun of an afternoon show can never be overrated. This is both old Vegas and new at its finest and usually for the right price. Please note: while the weather may not change much in Las Vegas, shows do.

Mac King

At Harrah's, 3475 Las Vegas Blvd. S. 800-392-9002, ext. 5222. www.mackingshow.com/ las-vegas.

Harrah's Entertainment Las Vegas

Mac King

If comedy-magic is your bag, then the Mac King Show, appearing afternoons in the Improv theater at Harrah's, is something you won't want to miss. King's unique act is not your run-of-the-mill magic show; it contains an unusual combination of quirky humor, visual gags, and amazing sleights of hand. Delivered in an hilarious tongue-in-cheek manner, it's serious magic.

Besides making his head disappear inside a paper bag, King fishes live goldfish out of the air, finds an audience member's playing card in a sealed box of cereal, transforms himself into Siegfried & Roy and then transforms Siegfried & Roy into a white tiger. Of course, the

King's Credits

King has appeared on seven NBC magic specials and holds the distinction of being the only performer to have performed on all five of NBC's *World's Greatest Magic* shows. He was most recently seen on the Late Show with David Letterman in 2008, and on Fox receiving an award for Best Comedy Magician at the 2007 World Magic Awards hosted by Sir Roger Moore.

audience is invited to participate. After the show, you can find King outside selling T-shirts and chatting with his fans.

King is known for his engaging personality and original illusions. Among them is his infamous Cloak of Invisibility, an ordinary yellow raincoat that possesses "extraordinary" powers.

King convinces the audience that this coat renders him invisible. The hilarious gag that follows involves astounding illusory feats.

The comedic magician also tosses his cookies—Fig Newtons—between the magical states of "now you see them" and "now you don't." King's affinity for Fig Newtons is a recurring sight gag in the show; the cookies seem to appear in the most unlikely places throughout his performance and disappear in the same manner—into his mouth or the mouths of audience members.

The Price is Right – Live!

At Bally's, 3645 Las Vegas Blvd. S.,
800-237-7469 or 702-967-4567
www.ballyslasvegas.com
Dark Sundays, Mondays.
Plays Friday at 7:30 pm;
All other days, 2:30 pm

Take an icon of American television history, put it on the Las Vegas stage and you are bound to get it right -- in this case "The Price is Right."

It's live. It's got the wit, the pace, and the prizes. What it does not have is the camera and Bob Barker. But Todd Newton, famed face from "E! News Live" and "Coming Attractions," keeps the show going with jokes and gags and models to make it pretty.

Aficionados of the show will recognize the pricing games: Cliff Hangers, Clock Game, Hole in One, Race Game, Plinko, It's in the Bag, and the Big Wheel, as contestants "come on down" and guess what common American consumer items cost. Prizes range from luggage to appliances to that "brand

new car"! Audience members must be 21 years old to be a contestant, pay the $49.50 admission and register at a booth located by the theater up to three hours before the show. Each of the 50 registrants receives a yellow price tag with their name. Players are chosen randomly for each round. Other audience members win Harrah's player points and other small prizes during the show. The thrills last 105 minutes, but for the lucky few they may last much longer.

The Price is Right – Live!

Gregory Popovich

At the V Theater in the Miracle Mile at Planet Hollywood, 3663 Las Vegas Blvd. S. 702-892-7790. www.varietytheater.com; www.comedypet.com.

It's animal house antics for this circus maestro-cum-cat juggler in his outrageous and hilarious afternoon pet show. All 15 cats and 10 dogs who jump through hoops for their master on stage were once strays. But Popovich shows that every dog can learn new tricks in a talented performance that takes his seasoned skills from his days as a juggler with Ringling Bros. and puts them into action with his favorite friends in an amusing afternoon show that's a one of a kind for Vegas, daily (*except Fri*) at 3:30 p.m.

Nathan Burton Comedy Magic

At the Flamingo Hotel and Casino, 3555 Las Vegas Blvd. S. 702-733-3333 or 888-902-9929. www.harrahs.com; www.nathanburton.com.

Nathan Burton brings afternoons to life in the Flamingo Showroom with his comedic ensemble of magic feats. Burton has been performing magic since the age of 4, but has managed to hone his act into a 60-minute whirlwind of in-your-face magical stunts blended with humor and, of course, showgirls. He received national attention recently when he took on the Ultimate Las Vegas Showgirl Challenge (2008) by spending seven nights inside a sealed box with seven showgirls—a stunt that received national attention from

E! Entertainment and CNN's Larry King. He also won a good deal of attention for the Miracle Mile Shops at Planet Hollywood Resort when he encased himself in a gigantic M-shaped ice sculpture in front of the mall on the Las Vegas Strip, joined by a rotating cast of bikini-clad showgirls inside the nine tons of ice. Visitors cruising The Strip could touch and inspect the 'M' and join in on the improbable occasion.

His show makes for an excellent midday diversion, at the "lost hour" of 4pm, as a warm up for a wild evening ahead.

Viva Las Vegas

At the Plaza Hotel & Casino, 1 Main St. 702-386-2110 or 800-634-6575. www.plazahotelcasino.com.

"Viva Las Vegas" is one of those Vegas shows that has been coming and going over the decades but continues to invoke the old Vegas-style humor for those lucky enough to see it. "Viva" opened at the Sands in April 1991, before moving to the Stratosphere in 1996 for its ten-year run. It's considered the city's longest-running daytime show.

The show still features its signature Elvis spoof and leggy, showgirly dancers, and then you have some numbers like Max Clever, the magician who has been seen on "Queer Eye for the Straight Guy," and uses his talent here for some fire-breathing illusions as well as cute dog tricks and comedy stunts between other acts. Still, for all its camp and circumstance, it's an engaging afternoon and a rare moment of Old Vegas.

MAGIC SHOWS

Now you see them... now you see them again and again and again. Las Vegas' resident headliner magicians have something up their sleeves indeed—tigers, women, birds, rocket ships and knives, to name a few. Faster than speeding bullets, able to leap tall reputations in a single bound, they are the supermen of the magic scene.

Amazing Johnathan

At Planet Hollywood
in the Harmon Theater,
3667 Las Vegas Blvd.
702-785-5555 or 866-919-PHRC
(7472). www.amazingj.com.

Seeing is believing, and nowhere is that truer than at Planet Hollywood, where the Amazing Johnathan appears every night but Wednesday and Thursday. From the moment the comedic magician walks out on stage, he offers a crystal-clear picture of bizarre comedy—while calmly gulping down Windex at any given moment.

With his bonafide don't-try-this-at-home act billed as "where magic and comedy collide," Johnathan focuses his impact on getting laughs. Nightly packed

It's Amazing

There are two real magic tricks in the Amazing Johnathan's show—the rest is spoof. Each of his shows is preceded by interactive audience comedy (via a live video camera and a *big* screen) and a different comedy or magic opening act weekly. During each show, Johnathan always brings up a "willing" participant on stage to assist him.

Parents beware: Johnathan does use profanity in his performance.

houses watch Johnathan eat razor blades, put a knife through his arm, put a pencil in his ear and out his nose, and swig Windex. Now, even without the help of his trusty assistant, the Psychic Tanya, Johnathan himself can see clearly into the future. And he's going to keep people laughing for a long time to come.

By his own admission, the acclaimed performer is as edgy and as politically incorrect as he can be. But he emphasizes that it's all in jest; he doesn't cross the line from funny to mean-spirited. His fast, furious and extremely funny approach has earned him rave reviews. Rolling Stone magazine refers to him as "one of the best comics working today." Among his honors, he is a two-time winner of the International Magic Award for "Best Comedy Magician."

Amazing Johnathan

Preferred Public Relations & Marketing

Lance Burton

*At the Monte Carlo Resort &
Casino, 3770 Las Vegas Blvd. S.
702-730-7777 or 877-311-8999.
www.lanceburton.com.*

Lance Burton was just five years
old when he became acquainted
with an illusion called the "Miser's
Dream." He was called up on stage
by magician Harry Collins, who
proceeded to pull silver dollars
from behind the young boy's ear,
his nose, under his chin and out
of thin air.

Collins then put the silver dollars
into a large bucket, which soon
overflowed with coins.

Of course, all that was just a drop
in the bucket compared with the
magical empire Burton would

Poof! It's Magic

Burton, who admits that it's the
plot or concept that he looks for
in deciding whether to do an illusion (he likes something with an
interesting twist at the end), has
become a master at putting his
own mark on the magic he performs. The magician tries not to
categorize his style and claims his
illusion-creating is a "mysterious
process" —even to him!

conjure up years later. But for
the master magician, that one
moment of magic changed his
life. Burton's goal in doing magic
is to give the audience the same
feeling he had when he was that
five-year-old boy.

Lance Burton

What's Up Burton's Sleeve?

- **Dove Act** – This famous act brought Burton to prominence. Burton makes
  doves appear and disappear, and vanish into handkerchiefs and candles.
- **Six-Pack** – Six beautiful showgirls come out of one suitcase in succession.
- **Floating Birdcage** – A birdcage holding Elvis the parakeet floats in mid-air
  three or four feet from Burton and then floats back.
- **The Flying Car** – A white Corvette flies in thin air, disappears, then reappears.
- **Sword Fight** – Burton's finale is a fencing match in which the magician
  fights a villain. It looks as though the bad guy kills Burton, but when the
  villain takes off his mask… voilà! It's Burton.

MAGIC SHOWS

🎩 Penn & Teller

At the Rio
700 W. Flamingo Rd.
702-777-7777 or 888-746-7784.
www.pennandteller.com.

The bad boys of magic, Penn & Teller always strive to make their audiences feel at home. That's because for this magical duo, home is where the wood chipper, handcuffs, razor blades, guns, and other props of their act are—it's wise to stay awake for this one! Luckily, home for Penn & Teller is at the Rio these days, where their act has become a permanent fixture (*nightly except Friday*), and the hotel happily cleans up the blood. The duo refers to themselves as "a couple of eccentric guys who have learned how to do a few cool things." *Newsweek* magazine described them as "pure entertainment and demented originality"; *Entertainment Weekly* dubbed them "two of the funniest people alive"; and David Letterman referred to the pair as "evil geniuses." However you view it, what you see is what you get with these two. Together since 1975, Penn & Teller are so-called "swindlers and scam

Penned and Teller-All
Penn & Teller have penned three best-selling books, *Cruel Tricks for Dear Friends, How to Play with Your Food* and *How to Play In Traffic.* They also have a popular series on the Showtime network.

artists" who perform tricks (and scams) with rather threatening props, not to mention the occasional bunny in a wood chipper. Their unique brand of magic and bizarre comedy includes throwing knives at attractive females in the audience, eating fire with a showgirl, transforming a wayward girl into an 800-pound gorilla; and hanging Penn by the neck while Teller does hand shadows. Vegas audiences force the pair to keep sharpening up their old tricks and coming up with new, more spectacular stunts. One can only imagine…

Teller's silent, creepy magic, mixed with Penn's clown and juggling expertise have taken the performers from street theatre to international fame and this regular slot at the Rio All-Suite Hotel & Casino.

Penn & Teller

Rio All-Suites and Hotel

MUST SEE

Dirk Arthur's Xtreme Magic

are showgirls and dancers and a variety of talents moving through the show, which runs twice daily, except Monday.

David Copperfield

At the MGM Grand,
3799 Las Vegas Blvd.
702-891-7777 or 877-880-0880.
www.dcopperfield.com

Master magician David Copperfield is a magician's magician who is well known for his amazing stunts, such as making the Statue of Liberty disappear. In his ongoing engagements at MGM Grand's Hollywood Theater he does not back down from his signature antics. For instance, rather than causing a great American icon to vanish, he turns the trick on himself, making himself disappear, reappear and his assistants do the same. As with his ghost-like walk through the Great Wall of China, he takes the feat to the stage by seeming to penetrate a solid block of metal.

Dirk Arthur's Xtreme Magic

At the Tropicana Hotel & Casino,
3801 Las Vegas Blvd.
702-739-2222 or 800-829-9034.
www. tropicanalv.com.

Dirk Arthur takes magic to extremes in his afternoon performances at the Tropicana in the Tiffany Showroom. And it's because of those extremes that the show is truly a show. Arthur is a prop magician, relying on elaborate props and showmanship for the real thrust of his magical entertainment.

The props do not get better than this: Bengal tigers, white-striped tigers, a pure white snow tiger, and black African leopards. He makes these man-eaters appear and disappear with the ease of a passing hand. An authentic 26-foot long Robinson helicopter also materializes out of the blue. Las Vegas is well known for its array of prop magician shows—Siegfried & Roy, David Copperfield—it takes a big stage and a lot of work to create these illusions. Naturally, there

Copperfield's hard-won illusions are grand enough to have earned him 21 television specials through the years. He has a place in the Guinness Book of World Records, nearly two dozen Emmys, even a star on Hollywood 's Walk of Fame. In Las Vegas his act includes such odd feats as the magician transporting himself and a member of the audience from the stage to a deserted island on the other side of the planet. At other times he makes whole swaths of the audience disappear. Plenty of audience participation is involved in this fast-paced and electrifying show.

GREAT IMPOSTERS

Some of Las Vegas' favorite performers just aren't themselves these days—everyone from Elvis to Neil Diamond to Kermit the Frog. These personalities suddenly have a doppelganger in the repertoire of the great impressionists—such as **Danny Gans**—who play Las Vegas. That's good news for nightlife.

American Superstars

At the Stratosphere,
2000 Las Vegas Blvd. S.
702-380-7777 or 800-998-6937.
www.stratlv.com.

American Superstars, since 1996 a highly touted celebrity impersonation show at the Stratosphere, got a buff makeover in the early years of the new millennium. In the process, the show itself took on a whole new personality—that of Elvis—who, having left it some time ago, is now back in the house, so to speak.

Mark Callas, executive producer of the show, and his partner, Donny Lee Moore, hadn't counted on a King at all. There hadn't been an Elvis in American Superstars since the show opened in Vegas at the Flamingo Hilton in 1993. Thereafter, sans Elvis, the show went to the Luxor from 1995 to 1997, and then opened at the Stratosphere (again without Elvis) in December 1997. Where public opinon was concerned, however, the King's absence at these venues was beginning to turn this theatrical property into a heartbreaker.

The show's repeat customers clamored for Elvis, who is definitely alive in Las Vegas thanks to any number of impersonators. So, beginning in 2000, the producers decided to refocus the show towards American pop icons, and Elvis was brought back in a big way. The show's been a smash hit ever since.

Since they're audience favorites, the acts in American Superstars don't change that often and you are likely to see Britney Spears, Tim McGraw, Michael Jackson and Christina among the celebrated

Preferred Public Relations & Marketing

Playing Among The Stars

American Superstars recently added an impression of the hard-rockin' Texas band ZZ Top to its lineup of musical celebrity tributes. The show includes Kevin Curry on guitar portraying Billy Gibbons, Dan Stover on bass as Dusty Hill and Craig Aaron Small on drums filling in for Frank Beard. ZZ Top catapulted to superstardom during the music-video era.

walk-ons. Everyone sings live, emulating the superstars they portray in voice, dress and mannerisms.

🎵 Barbra and Frank, The Concert That Never Was

At the Riviera Hotel & Casino, 2901 Las Vegas Blvd. S. 702-734-5110 or 800-634-6753. www.theriviera.com.

Las Vegas may be known for its super-sized resorts and its over-the-top faux architecture and attractions, but it's also the world's epicenter for celebrity imposter acts. One must-see example is Barbra and Frank, The Concert That Never Was, at the Riviera's Le Bistro Lounge.
The mismatched duo of Sharon Owens and Sebastian Anzaldo make something that might never have worked—a concert featuring Barbra Streisand and Frank Sinatra—into a good show, with some hokey comedic numbers and lots of good crooning. The moody,

cigarette-toting chairman indulging in witty repartee with the motor-mouthed heroine of *Funny Girl* is in itself an act to behold, and it's made ever more charming with the lineup of sentimental songs and fine piano accompaniment. The tribute opens with both performers singing "I've Got A Crush On You" à la the 1993 Duets album. They depart into solos and return again for more banter at the piano, lapsing into such tunes as "Witchcraft," "Bewitched, Bothered and Bewildered," "You Don't Bring Me Flowers" and build up to the "New York, New York" crescendo. Among Frank's solo numbers are "I've Got The World On A String," "Summer Wind," "Come Fly With Me," "Fly Me To The Moon," and "My Way."
Anzaldo as Sinatra brings the audience to their feet with a moving rendition of "That's Life."

🎵 Danny Gans

At The Mirage, 3400 Las Vegas Blvd. S. 702-791-7111 or 800-627-6667. www.dannygans.com.

One look at Danny Gans on stage and it's easy to see why he has become the Vegas ideal. He's talented, he's witty, and he's just loaded with personalities—nearly 300 of them, to be exact. Not to mention that he's always the lives *(sic.)* of the party, the one he invites people to attend five nights a week in The Danny Gans Theatre at the Mirage. He opened here in April 2000 to consistently sold-out crowds. He moves to Encore at Wynn at the beginning of 2009. Nicknamed "the man of a thousand voices," he's truly a man for all

Barbra and Frank

Riviera Hotel & Casino

Gans' show offers an entire spectrum of entertainment, taking people from the 1940s with favorites Frank Sinatra, Tony Bennett and Nat King Cole to current recording artists such as John Meyer, Macy Gray and Dave Matthews. In his emotional portrayal of Bruce Springsteen singing "The Rising," Gans not only sings but plays the guitar, too. His acting piece, which includes scenes from *On Golden Pond*, *Rocky*, *Forrest Gump* and *Scent of a Woman*, has garnered raves from the likes of Sylvester Stallone, Kevin Costner and Dustin Hoffman.

ages. Chronological ages, that is. His show, which is different every night, offers about 100 fast-paced impressions of singing stars and actors from every age group and era, leaving no tone unturned. The crowd doesn't even seem to mind that every so often, when Gans opens his mouth to sing, he obviously has a little frog in his throat. Not to worry, it's only Kermit. Like his Muppet friend, Gans has found his own "rainbow connection" with his audiences.

🎭 An Evening at La Cage

At the Riviera Hotel & Casino, 2901 Las Vegas Blvd. S. 702-734-5110 or 800-634-6753. www.theriviera.com; www.frankmarino.com.

You could say that for nearly half of his 40+ years, life has been a drag for Frank Marino. He stars nightly as comedienne Joan Rivers in *An Evening at La Cage*. Celebrating his 20th anniversary in 2005 with the famed female impersonation show, Marino has always been "one of the guys who's one of the girls." There's no denying that Marino, who's had more than $100,000 worth of plastic surgery, looks better in an evening gown than most women. Now he's ready to come out of the closet—the one, that is, holding his extravagant wardrobe and jewelry. Here's someone with every reason to be perfectly frank about what it takes to be a woman in a man's world: "Can we talk?"

Marino makes 17 costume changes a night. His closet contains a

What's Up Doc? Danny Gans

MGM Grand/Mirage

60

Frankly Speaking

Marino gets some of his material from some very unique sources. When it comes to the designs for his gowns, 90 percent of the time he dreams up the ideas and the rest come from some offbeat sources. One of those places is from the Barbie doll, which the impersonator claims has the best fantasy dresses. Marino quips that he is actually a copy of Barbie, "the only one who has more plastic parts than him."

host of gowns, which range in price from $1,000 to $5,000 apiece, and he pays for every one himself. Designed mainly by costume king Bob Mackie, Marino's wardrobe has become such a trademark over the years that people come to the show just to see his new outfits. Although he opens the show as Joan Rivers, Marino does the rest of the changes as a glamorous femme fatale character.

Legends In Concert

At the Imperial Palace,
3535 Las Vegas Blvd. S.
702-731-3311 or 800-634-6441.
www.imperialpalace.com.

Frank Sinatra still comes around to perform; Richie Valens pops in to entertain; and Elvis has not left the building in two decades. Deceased though these celebrities may be,

their impersonations and those of others live on, brought together in this show. Contemporary performers impersonate those celebs that time has lost, as well as those still with us—legends dead and alive are brought to life nightly in the Imperial Palace's celebrity tribute show, Legends In Concert, which celebrated its 22nd anniversary in May 2005.

Considered the granddaddy of the live-star impersonation shows, Legends in Concert is not only

> Frank Marino has been voted "Best Dressed in Las Vegas" repeatedly. It's no wonder with what he has to choose from:
> - 2,000 evening gowns
> - A trunk full of jewelry
> - 50 wigs
> - 300 pairs of shoes

Frank Marino and Friends

Riviera Hotel & Casino

the original show of this type, but it's far and away the biggest. The show changes every three months. The list of nearly 100 legends portrayed over the years includes Marilyn Monroe, Buddy Holly, Madonna, Jerry Lee Lewis, The Beatles, Dean Martin and Jennifer Lopez.

The Rat Pack is Back

At the Plaza Hotel & Casino,
1 Main Street.
702-386-2444 or 800-634-6575.
www.plazahotelcasino.com.

This two-hour tribute to the Rat Pack (Frank Sinatra, Sammy Davis Jr., Dean Martin, Joey Bishop and Peter Lawford), with a cameo by Marilyn Monroe, starts off with a voice-over introduction by Buddy Hackett. The show then brings on Hackett's real-life son, Sandy, in the role of Joey Bishop to start the roll of gags, jokes, songs and continuous sipping in this re-creation of the Copa Room show at the erstwhile Sands Hotel.

They've modernized the show (the racial barbs at Davis have softened) and they try to give an even hand to the different players, each of whom performs key musical numbers and acts that reflect his career. Of course, there's still the infamous drink cart, the constant kidding, and magical chemistry similar to that shared by the real Rat Pack.

The show comes with dinner in true Old Vegas fashion.

Formerly at the Greek Isles, show's new home at the Plaza (a property that seems lodged in the '70s) is the perfect place for this spoofing group to call home for now.

Fab Four Mania

At Planet Hollywood Resort's V Theater, 3667 Las Vegas Blvd. S.
702-932-1818 or 877-33-9474.
www.varietytheater.com.

Beatles are big in Vegas whether played out as interpretive and impossible ballet moves on a theater in the round or by four zanie mop tops having the time of their lives on stage. The Fab Four production at Planet Hollywood might be described as Beatles-lite compared with the pomp and circumstance of Cirque choreography seen at the Mirage. But this lean and mean musical review is full of fun for the Beatlemaniacs among us. The show is full of jokes and joshing with each other and the audience between riffs into favorite numbers. Because it is four guys who do a good job of matching the qualities of the Beatle they play, the performance has energy and, for a suspended moment, even feels like the real thing.

Tribute to Neil Diamond

At the Riviera,
2901 Las Vegas Blvd.
702-794-9433 or 877-892-7469.
www.rivierahotel.com.

You may not be able to see the great rock balladeer, Neil Diamond, up close and in this lifetime, but you can catch his likeness at the Riviera most nights in Le Bistro Theater. The show features Jay White, who was Jazz Singer through the 1990s in the Legends in Concert show at the IP. Complete in sparkle garb and open white shirt, he belts Diamond's 60s hits in performances that earn standing ovations.

Wayne Brady: Making it Up

At The Venetian,
3355 Las Vegas Blvd.
702-414-9000 or 877-883-6423.
www.waynebrady.com.

From the famous 90s show, "Whose Line is it Anyway" with Drew Carey, to the fabulous one-man headlining show at the Venetian, Wayne Brady has had a charmed career. The multi-talented stage force has all the polish of Ben Vereen but takes his show to unpredictable places each night, adlibbing all the way. He had a lot of practice at this genre during his television tenure. The show centered on four performers who would create skits, scenes and songs on the spot according to topics raised by the audience. Brady has since moved through his own televised talk shows to Comedy Central's Chappelle's Show to become a force among the progressive voices of comedy and satire, especially in the leagues of Spike Lee, Wanda Sykes, DL Hughley, and Paul Mooney. Talent and versatility prevent Brady from fitting squarely into any hole. At the Venetian's Showroom Brady keeps the entertainment piqued with spontaneous skits and performances, plus songs from his own line-up of hits.

Soprano's Last Supper

At the Riviera Comedy Club,
2901 Las Vegas Blvd.
702-733-8669 or 800-944-5639.
www.sopranosvegas.com.

A night with the Sopranos is like Tony 'n Tina's wedding on steroids. Time spent with "the Family" is anything but easy as this Sopranos recreation puts the audience right in the scene of one of HBO's finest series. The characters are established through the first act, which is played off a script and introduces the plot. Afterwards anything goes as it is all ad-libbed and the audience is invited to Tony Baritone's (T's alias after he has moved his family out to Vegas) indictment party. Things pick up as the meal progresses through fabulous zitis and lasagnas (yes, this is one of the few dinner shows in town) and spectators become more family than, perhaps, they ever wanted to be. The room takes on the life of a genuine supper club, not a multi-purpose hotel space. A band onstage plays and people dance. A crooner belts "I've Got You Under My Skin." The only thing missing perhaps is Uncle Jun grabbing the mic and bringing the mood down to the Old Country. Bring an appetite, leave your belief system back in the room and join the party.

George Wallace

At the Flamingo,
3555 Las Vegas Blvd.
702-733-3333 or 888-902-9929.
www.georgewallace.com.

Part gospel revival, part Red Foxx redux, George Wallace keeps audiences singing and laughing and tapping through a very entertaining 90 minutes in a show that is different every night. The talk and comedy part of the show pokes fun at everyday situations, lands a litany of "Yo Mama" jokes but stays entertaining all the while.

GREAT IMPOSTERS

63

ANIMAL ACTS

Some of the best acts in Vegas have fins and fur. These animals love the bright lights and know how to claw—or swim—their way to the top. The best part is, they work for food!

Shark Reef

★★Shark Reef

At Mandalay Bay,
3950 Las Vegas Blvd. S.
702-632-7777 or 877-632-7400.
www.sharkreef.com.
Open year-round daily
10am–11pm. $16.95 adults,
$10.95 children (ages 5-12;
ages 4 & under free).

Just when you thought it was safe to go back into the casino, along comes an adventure that grips you in the "Jaws" of excitement. Shark Reef at Mandalay Bay is not your typical aquarium. This total sensory experience takes you on a journey through an ancient temple that

has been slowly claimed by the sea. You wind up on the deck of a sunken treasure ship in shark-infested waters.

Developed in consultation with the Vancouver Aquarium Marine Science Center in Vancouver, Canada—one of the world's most respected marine facilities—the 90,560-square-foot Shark Reef is home to a diverse cross-section of magnificent aquatic creatures, including different species of sharks, exotic fish, stingrays, reptiles and turtles. Featuring more than 2,000 specimens, the reef holds nearly 1.6 million gallons of seawater among its 14 exhibits.

Treasure Bay – Meet four different species of sharks—tiger, sandbar, lemon and nurse—along with majestic green sea turtles and a variety of fish.
Crocodile Habitat – Encounter rare golden crocodiles, a hybrid between saltwater and Siamese crocs.
Lizard Lounge – Get up close to 9-foot-long monitor lizards—if you dare.
Touch Pool – Discover what shark skin really feels like, examine the shell of a horseshoe crab, and learn how sea stars swim along the ocean floor.

★The Lion Habitat

At the MGM Grand,
3799 Las Vegas Blvd. S.
877-880-0880.
www.mgmgrand.com.
Open year-round daily
11am–10pm. Free.

MGM Grand guarantees visitors the lion's share of excitement at the hotel's renowned Lion Habitat. Located inside the casino next to Studio 54, the tri-story structure showcases a variety of African lions and cubs, including Goldie, Metro and Baby Lion (a direct descendant of MGM Studio's signature marquee lion, Metro).

Besides adding an adventurous element to the hotel, the lion habitat truly educates guests about these magnificent creatures. You'll see lions up, down and all around as they romp throughout the $9 million, 5,345-square-foot structure, which is enclosed by glass and encased by skylights. The habitat boasts 35-foot-high walls, allowing visitors the opportunity to watch the lions' every move; and move they do. The lions can prowl above and below you at any time, via a see-through

To Ride With Lions

Evans transports lions from his property, which is 12 miles from the MGM Grand, to the hotel two to three times a day. Accustomed to humans, and comfortable in front of a camera, the felines are at home being up-close and personal with their human counterparts. There are between one and five animals in the habitat at any given period; no group stays in the structure for more than six hours at a time.

walkway tunnel running through the habitat. Veteran animal trainer Keith Evans owns, oversees and trains the animals. He also helped design the habitat.

Adorned with trees and foliage, and featuring four waterfalls, multiple overhangs and a pond, the habitat is designed to be a splendid and humane showcase for the majestic creatures. Admission is free but you can take your photo with lions nearby and shop at the habitat gift store where a portion of the purchase will go to lion preservation.

Lion Habitat at the MGM Grand

★The Secret Garden of Siegfried & Roy

At The Mirage,
3400 Las Vegas Blvd. S.
702-791-7111 or 800-627-6667.
www.miragehabitat.com.
Open Mon–Fri 11am–5:30pm,
Sat–Sun 10am–5:30pm. $15
adults, $10 children (ages 4-12).

It's probably the best-kept secret in town. Lush manicured grass, graceful palm trees, bright flowers, and crystal-clear waterfalls and pools abound within the borders of this ethereal place. In the background, the calls of exotic birds and jungle drums play over loudspeakers. You may hear a few roars now and then, but that's just the garden's feline residents itching to share with the public the great news about this 15-acre wildlife refuge. That is, what the founders of the place, world-renowned illusionists Siegfried & Roy, for years Las Vegas' best-known headliners, most cherish about it: that some of the world's rarest animals live here in harmony with one another and with humans.

White Tigers

White with black stripes, pink paws and pale blue eyes, white tigers are are not albinos. They are a genetic variation that lacks dark pigmentation. White tigers born in the wild rarely survive because they lack the natural camouflage that hides them from their enemies.

More than 70 animals reside within the sanctuary, including white tigers, white lions, Bengal tigers, panthers and snow leopards. With only chain-link fences separating animal from human, the $13 million jungle habitat showcases these beasts in their natural environment with ample amounts of space for play and exercise. Behind the garden, unseen by the public, there's an indoor-outdoor compound the size of two football fields that includes catwalks 100 feet in length for exercise purposes and an air-conditioned structure housing an animal hospital, clinic and nursery.

It's a quiet place of wonder here, a Secret Garden, indeed.

Secret Garden of
Siegfried & Roy

MUST SEE

The Atlantis Aquarium

At The 🖼 **Forum Shops** *at Caesar's Palace, 3570 Las Vegas Blvd. S. 702-893-3807. www.robertwynn.com/FishAq.htm. Tours available daily at 1:15pm & 5:15pm.*

"Don't bite the hand that feeds you" is the golden rule at the Atlantis Aquarium, where you can watch divers feed the fish twice daily. The backdrop to the **Lost City of Atlantis** animatronic statue show, this 50,000-gallon marine aquarium contains a variety of brightly colored tropical fish. The standout notables among the species, however, are the sharks and stingrays.

Make sure you drop by at 3:15pm or 7:15pm, when you can witness the feeding frenzy as divers enter the tank. The aquarium offers a below-the-scenes tour of the support facilities during the week *(dive shows & tours are free of charge).*

The Dolphin Habitat

At The Mirage, 3400 Las Vegas Blvd. S. 702-791-7111 or 800-627-6667. www.themirage.com. Open Mon–Fri, 11am–5:30pm, weekends 10am–5:30pm. $15 adults, $10 children (ages 4-12). Admission includes Secret Garden of Siegfried & Roy.

Adjoining Siegfried and Roy's tropical Secret Garden, behind the Mirage, the Dolphin Habitat makes a huge splash with visitors year after year. Its purpose is to provide a sanctuary for Atlantic bottlenose dolphins and to educate the public about marine mammals and their environment. It's also a research and breeding facility. The

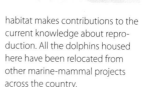

A Fish Story
- More than 500 individual fish representing more than 100 species inhabit the Atlantis Aquarium.
- The fish range in size from two inches to a 4-foot-long nurse shark, the largest in the aquarium.

habitat makes contributions to the current knowledge about reproduction. All the dolphins housed here have been relocated from other marine-mammal projects across the country.

Wildlife Habitat

At the Flamingo Las Vegas. 3555 Las Vegas Blvd. S. 702-733-3111 or 800-732-2111. www.flamingolasvegas.com. Open year-round 24 hours. Free.

The Flamingo, once the secret home of Bugsy Siegel and Virginia Hill, is now the habitat of an assortment of exotic birds, fish and turtles, which hang out around a comely rock pond and a 15-acre tropical garden near the pool. See live Chilean flamingoes and an assemblage of koi, tortoises and swans, all free for the observing. Be sure to come by at 8:30am and 3pm for feeding time.

MGM Grand/Mirage

Give us a hand… Dolphin Habitat

ANIMAL ACTS

WEDDING CHAPELS

Getting hitched Vegas-style can make saying "I do" as easy as buying a burger or as elaborate as an episode of HBO's 2005 series *Rome*. With nearly 130,000 marriage licenses issued last year, someone ties the knot here every 14 minutes (that rate doubles on New Year's Eve and triples on Valentine's Day).

Little White Chapel

Brian Jones

How can you join the fun? All you need is proof of age (a driver's license, passport or birth certificate); a social security number (foreigners who exchange wedding vows in the US may need special documentation to guarantee the marriage is recognized in their country); parental consent; a court order (if participants are under age 16); and $55 for the license. No blood test. No waiting period. *For details, contact Clark County Marriage License Bureau (200 South Third St., 1st floor; 702-455-4416 or 702-455-4415; www.co.clark.nv.us/clerk/marriage_information.htm).* Whether you want to get married by Elvis, elope like Cleopatra or dash off your vows with your morning coffee, there are more than 50 chapels to do the job. Most Strip resorts have at least one chapel, and often two or three, with a full staff of wedding experts to help with the planning. These can be simple to elaborate ceremonies and in some lush and floral settings near pools and falls.

Wild, Wild Weddings

Las Vegas offers no shortage of creative ways to get married. Here are a few suggestions for one-of-a-kind nuptials:

- Get married on a gondola with a serenading gondolier at The Venetian.
- Have a pirate swoop down to deliver your rings as you are pronounced man and wife on a tattered and tough pirates' ship at TI.
- Say "I do" 1,000 feet above The Strip at Stratosphere Tower.
- Have a Roman wedding, complete with sentries and sultry slave girls, at Caesars Palace.
- Crash your own wedding in a Pink Cadillac driven by and then officiated by Elvis at Viva Las Vegas Wedding Chapel.
- Get married with George Clooney or Brad Pitt or Jennifer Lopez at your side at Madame Tussaud's. Say "I do" by your favorite best man and maid of honor—there are more than 100 waxen celebrities to pick from. A $1,200 package can manage it all, from the limo rides and rose bouquets to wedding photos with the men and women of your dreams.

Other settings, such as the **Little White Chapel**, built in 1950 near downtown Las Vegas, remain a favorite for their kitschiness. It has half-a-dozen pews, an Elvis officiante on call, and a Tunnel of Vows, where for a $40 ride you can become husband and wife *(1301 Las Vegas Blvd.; 702-382-5943 or 800-545-8111; www.littlewhite chapel.com)*.

Viva Las Vegas Chapel

1205 Las Vegas Blvd.
702-384-0771 or 800-574-4450.
www.vivalasvegas.com.

Elvis is always at the ready in the Viva Las Vegas Wedding Chapel. This former motel has two traditional chapels and several smaller themed locations that can be put to use on that wedding day. These include the '50s diner room, complete with juke box and soda fountain, the gazebo and the garden. Within any chosen venue, VLV can dress it up for a kitschy wedding party. Cookie cutter ceremonies include Elvis Blue Hawaii, Beach Party, the Egyptian Tut Hut, Rocky Horror, Liberace—just name your favorite fantasy scene. The chapel keeps yarmulkes and rings on hand and a picture perfect pink '50s Caddie convertible to rush couples—or fools—into their special ceremony.

Graceland Chapel

619 Las Vegas Blvd.
702-382-0091 or 800-824-5732.
www.gracelandchapel.com.

Naturally, Elvis is the key to this chapel, which claims to be the one that started it all—Elvis Nuptials, that is. Traditional weddings can also happen in this chapel that looks more like a church in the meadows than something from Graceland. Celebs to tie the knot here include Bon Jovi, Billy Ray Cyrus and Aaron Neville.

Little Church of the West

4617 Las Vegas Blvd.
702-739-7971 or 800-821-2452.
www.littlechurchlv.com.

Dating back to 1942, this church has seen it all in Las Vegas. The second oldest church in town (after Wee Kirk o' the Heather) still retains its original charms in all the original settings. It's a simple wooden abode with a steeple in an arbored yard, but it can hold 50 inside, although there's ne'er an Elvis in sight. Famed "I dos" include Zsa Zsa Gabor and George Sanders, Judy Garland, Mickey Rooney, Dudley Moore, Richard Gere and Cindy Crawford. Britney Spears even married here in 2004 for all of 55 hours, before having the "joke" marriage annulled.

A Special Memory Wedding Chapel

800 S. Fourth St.
702-384-2211 or 800-962-7798.
www.aspecialmemory.com.

If you really can't wait, this is the chapel for you. No fuss, no muss, you can even stay in your car. The chapel performs "drive-thru" ceremonies for $25 (plus $40 for the minister). It also offers sit-down services with interior spaces for up to 110 guests, and an outdoor gazebo for smaller affairs.

WEDDING CHAPELS

VEGAS FOR FREE

Who says you can't get something for nothing? Some of the best things in life are free in Las Vegas. That includes the pleasures derived from the city's many physical attractions—at least those of the inanimate variety…

Bellagio Fountains

★★Bellagio Fountains

At Bellagio, 3600 Las Vegas Blvd. S. 702-693-7111 or 888-987-6667. www.bellagioresort.com.

The Fountains of Bellagio are undoubtedly the big shot of The Strip. Twice an hour (or, at night, every 15 minutes) the 1,100 fountains shoot as high as 240 feet into the air, choreographed to music including everything from the classic arias of Luciano Pavarotti to show tunes, and from Liberace to the romantic stylings of Frank Sinatra. More than a thousand fountains dance in front of the hotel. At just barely under 20 million gallons and 8.5 acres, Lake Bellagio is easily the largest musical fountain system in the world. Watch it from across the street—a sidewalk table at Paris' Mon Ami Gabi speaks romance.

Bellagio Conservatory and Botanical Gardens★

Just beyond the lobby at Bellagio, you'll find the lovely conservatory garden with its 50-foot-high glass ceiling. The ceiling framework and beams are sculpted in floral patterns from -oxidized copper, called verde. With the change of each season, the garden puts on a different face, with new trees and flowers. It also puts on spectacular displays for Thanksgiving, Christmas and the Chinese New Year.

Bellagio Conservatory

★★Fremont Street Experience

425 Fremont St. 702-678-5777.
www.vegasexperience.com.

If you're traveling downtown from The Strip, it may feel like Las Vegas has disappeared somewhere between St. Louis Avenue and Fremont Street. Don't give up, just keep on going and you'll definitely see the light. Or lights, in this case—more than two million light bulbs to be exact, down on Fremont Street.

Since it opened in December 1995, the Fremont Street Experience has turned up the wattage in downtown Las Vegas every night with a spectacular computer-generated sound-and-light show. The Experience is a modern technological and engineering marvel, clearly one of a kind. Suspended 90 feet over downtown, a four-acre barrel-arched canopy jolts to life several times nightly above a four-block section of Fremont Street *(between Main & 4th Sts.)*. Holding it aloft are 16 columns, each weighing 26,000 pounds and each capable of bearing 400,000 pounds. The illuminated extravaganza of flashing, rolling images is generated by more than two million fiber-optic lights and synchronized to music from a 540,000-watt sound system. Created by a consortium of 11 casinos, the attraction has transformed downtown's five-block principal thoroughfare into a mix of urban theater and a variety of dining, entertainment and shopping venues. Under its high dome, the canopy creates a pedestrian mall closed to traffic and encompassing several of Las Vegas' most popular downtown casinos, including the Golden Nugget.

"Watts" up on Fremont Street?
- 180 computer-programmed, high-intensity strobe lights
- 64 variable-color lighting fixtures that can produce 300 colors
- 8 robotic mirrors per block that can be individually programmed to pan and tilt to reflect light

★★Mirage Volcano

At The Mirage,
3400 Las Vegas Blvd. S.
702-791-7111 or 800-627-6667.
www.themirage.com.

The Mirage volcano, no longer a mere 54 foot leap of middling flames, is now an immersive

Brian Jones, Las Vegas News Bureau/LVCVA

Fremont Street Experience Show

Mirage Volcano

The Mirage

explosion of fire, water and sound that will simply take your breath away—possibly steaming it first. With a recent $25 million magma lift (that debuted in December 2008), the iconic Strip volcano more than doubled its incendiary reach to 120 and also doubled its running time to 4.5 minutes. New 'FireShooters' designed by WET (think Bellagio fountains, Bellagio Conservatory, the fountains for 1998 Lisboa Expo, the cauldron for the 2002 Olympic Winter Games), plus new water design and steam elements, a rock design for the volcano and an expanded meandering tropical lagoon makes for a traffic stopper and crowd pleaser that only Las Vegas could execute. The icing on this cake (shall we say plume of this caldera?) is the music. Beyond the mesmerizing conflagration is a percussive build to a riveting crescendo composed by legendary Grateful Dead drummer Micky Hart and Indian Tabla sensation Zakir Hussain. The seven-movement oeuvre contains indigenous music and soundscapes recorded from around the world and some one-of-a-kind instruments heard nowhere else. Timed to complement the performances of the Sirens of TI, crowds packing along this mid-Strip stretch will not be disappointed.

72

The Sirens of TI

At Treasure Island,
3300 Las Vegas Blvd. S.
702-894-7111 or 800-944-7444.
www.treasureislandlasvegas.com.

Since its inception, *The Pirate Battle of Buccaneer Bay at Treasure Island* was always what the name implied—a 12-minute fight to the finish between a British frigate, the HMS *Britannia*, and a pirate ship, the *Hispaniola*.

In tandem with the hotel's tenth anniversary in 2003, a new show called *The Sirens of TI* was unveiled. A sensual, modern interpretation of the Pirate Battle, male pirates are now joined by female sirens, who are part muse, part seductress and part pirate. Directed and choreographed by Kenny Ortega (of *Dirty Dancing* fame), the show is a modern pop musical with singing, dancing, feats of amazing strength, pyrotechnics and sound. Ortega claims that ancient Greece's legendary sirens were his inspiration for the storyline.

Sirens of TI

Treasure Island

🎪 Circus Circus Big Top

At Circus Circus Hotel & Casino, 2880 Las Vegas Blvd. S. 702-734-0410 or 877-634-3450. www.circuscircus.com.

Festival of Fountains

Caesars Palace

When this property opened in 1968 it was a first for Vegas—a hotel that provided something for kids to do while their parents gambled. It's still a unique destination along The Strip. A literal three-ring circus, which bills itself as the world's largest permanent circus, surrounds the casino with real circus acts performed day and night. Even hardcore slot-pullers take a break to watch the trapeze artists swing from the heights above them. Dazzling aerialists, trapeze artists, magicians, contortionists and clowns shows are just a few of the myriad performers that give shows free-of-charge twice an hour daily, from 11am to midnight. Catch the spectacular juggling feats of renowned performers who hail from Moscow and Moldavian circus troupe as well as the acrobatic, trapeze and aerialists antics of The Sandou Troupe. The acts change, so you will see different feats if you come back later.

Festival Fountain Show

At The 🛍 Forum Shops at Caesars Palace, 3570 Las Vegas Blvd. S. 702-893-4800. www.harrahs.com.

You can't help but be amazed at the new level of animatronics and laser lighting that the Festival of Fountains boasts. The party starts at 10am, when Bacchus, god of wine, wakes up and decides to throw a party for himself. He enlists the powers of Apollo, god of music; Venus, goddess of love; and Plutus, god of wealth. As the festivities begin, the statues talk and move, enhanced by animatronics and laser special effects. The entire show is controlled by computer. Each statue's voice is a scripted recording that runs on a cue list that "talks" to the computer. There are over 700 cues for one entire show, which lasts eight minutes—the memory of it lasts much longer. A second dramatic fountain show of exploding fire and ice runs hourly in the middle wing of the complex.

Masquerade Show in the Sky

At the Rio, 3700 W. Flamingo Rd. 702-777-7777 or 800-752-9746. www.riolasvegas.com.

A $25-million interactive entertainment experience, Masquerade Show in the Sky reflects the spirit of Brazil's Carnivale. The show consists of five complete parades—Village Street Party, South of the

Border, Carnivale, Venice Masquerade and New Orleans Mardi Gras, which alternate throughout the day. Each 12-minute show has different music, costumes and performances by a 26-member cast. Five performer-filled floats, each boasting its own individually themed music and sound system, move on a 950-foot track 13 feet above the casino floor of Masquerade Village. For a small fee, you can dress in costume and climb aboard one of the floats to cavort with the entertainers. There is a catch—and hopefully it's yours as the entertainers throw out bright strands of beads from the floats to the crowds below.

Neon Museum

East end of Fremont Street Experience, downtown.
702-387-6366.
www.neonmuseum.org.
Open year-round 24 hours.

The Neon Museum was erected in 1996 out of the ashes of the Neon Boneyard, where all good electric signs must someday go to die. A living, outdoor exhibition area on the far side of the Fremont Street Experience, the museum takes visitors on a sentimental walking journey, past the famed Hacienda Hotel's horseman and the golden bulbs of Aladdin's Lamp (from the original Aladdin Hotel structure) to the c. 1961 Flame Restaurant sign, pulsing on the roof of the restaurant once located on Desert Inn Road. You'll also see the Chief Hotel Court sign from the 1940s, when the hotel was located on that street. The corridor continues along the pedestrian corridor of Fremont Street and is dotted with odd souvenir and notion shops and the more recent Neonopolis mall and theater complex.

Town Square

6605 Las Vegas Blvd. S.
www.townsquarelasvegas.com

Land is eminently available and relatively inexpensive as you inch south of The Strip toward LA. The newest shopping center to emerge in this developer's heaven is the eighth such mega mall to grace Las Vegas Blvd. between Spring Mountain and Warm Springs roads. The sprawling 1.5 million sq ft development claims to be a "lifestyle center," and indeed this small town of big chain stores offers a slice of life on Main Street Barcelona, Main Street Milan, Main Street Casablanca and Main Street San Diego. The developers have tried to side-step the uniformity of your usual model town by injecting, Botox style, some 70 different "façade types," into the architecture.

Vegas' familiar promenades and skyscrapers give way here to small tree-lined streets—with parking meters ($1/hr)—and two-story buildings. Over 150 shops, more than a dozen restaurants and several entertainment venues keep it all interesting.

The lengthy list of retailers includes The Strip's second Apple Store. Diners will find Tommy Bahamas Tropical Café intriguing; shop for shirts then sip Mai Tais on the patio overlooking the park. Yes, there is a park, just a like a real town, or a Vegas town at least. This 9,000-square-foot patch is the centerpiece of the project with a hedge maze, a 25-foot high tree house, pop-up fountains, a Tom Sawyer house, a mini replica of the center, storytelling stages and plenty of park benches for tired mall rats.

Fremont Street East

5th to 7th Streets along Fremont St.

Downtown Vegas is experiencing a retro renaissance. Once you've had your ten minutes of bedazzlement watching the corridor canopy of Fremont Street's "Vivavision," head to the Downtown territory known as Fremont Street East, along Fremont. This is the city's arthouse entertainment district where bohemian denizens flock to such hot spots as The Beauty Bar *(517 Fremont St., 702-598-1965, www.beautybar.com)*, well-known to Angelenos for its Hollywood flagship. It swells with vintage interiors: beauty stations for pedicures and Pernod, a genre-embracing soundtrack and a funky back door patio. Next door is the Griffin *(511 Fremont St., (702) 382-0577)*, a dark, somewhat goth, drinking establishment with a central fireplace and castle-like motifs. The promenade brings plenty of vintage Vegas neon with it and extends an area of Fremont Street that has seen a proliferation of up-market and casual scene bars and restaurants in recent years. Watch for the old, bulb-busting Silver Slipper shoe—all aglow again.

Beyond Buskers

You don't have to wander the streets of Venice or Las Ramblas of Barcelona to see human statues masking as fine art. The **Canal Shoppes** at the Venetian has taken a tip from its European counterparts and put their own street artists to work creating a mall gallery of human statuary and lively street performance. They call it "Streetmosphere" here, but unlike the ambient cobbled sidewalks of the old country, no hats are passed. You need not shell out those quarters and dollars to hear a trio of tenors dressed in Renaissance garb breaking into a familiar aria or two. Stay around as long as you like. There is even a St. Mark's Square where you can have your latte and gelato and not have to shoo away the bird life while watching a steady stream of artists entertain.

MUSEUMS

It has often been said that good things come in small packages. So it is with Nevada's museums and art galleries. Although Las Vegas is hardly known for its museums, the city has come a long way in equipping itself with unique museum offerings.

★★The Atomic Testing Museum

755 E. Flamingo Rd.
702-794-5161.
www.atomictestingmuseum.org.
Open year-round Mon–Sat
9am–5pm, Sun 1pm–5pm.
Closed Jan 1, Thanksgiving Day
& Dec 25. $12.

Las Vegas may be ground zero for the largest hotels on the planet, but did you know it was also ground zero for friendly nukes from 1951 to 1992?

This well-curated museum, designed with assistance from the Smithsonian Institution, recounts the history of atomic testing in the US—the good, the bad, and the ugly—through newsreel videos, painstakingly detailed environmental re-creations, and brilliantly interpreted explanations. You'll even get to experience a simulated atomic explosion from the confines of a sealed underground room (not for the claustrophobic). What's so impressive about the 8,000-square-foot space tucked into the Desert Research Institute is not so much what you see, but the resources that are available at every turn.

From the library to the gift shop, you'll find former test-site employees and engineers eager to talk about the reality of life on that off-limits, 1,400-square-mile, pock-marked, radioactive preserve located 65 miles northwest of Las Vegas, and debunk the myths that continue to swirl around the secrecy of operations there.

★★Bellagio Gallery of Fine Art

3600 Las Vegas Blvd. S.
702-693-7919. www.bellagio.
com. Open year-round Mon–Fri
10am–6pm (Fri, Sat until 9pm).
$15 (includes audio tour). Reservations strongly advised.

Atomic Testing Museum

Bellagio Gallery of Fine Art

With the creation of the Bellagio Gallery of Fine Art, the first gallery on The Strip, it became clear that art in Las Vegas was no longer being given the brush-off. The facility is a noncommercial venue dedicated to presenting high-quality art exhibitions from major national and international museums. It generally brings in two exhibitions a year from the world's greatest art collections, each on display for a period of six months. Past exhibits have included the works of Andy Warhol, Alexander Calder and Peter Carl Fabergé. The gallery offers a self-guided audio tour, so you can stop before any painting and listen to the details about that particular work.

★The Auto Collections

At the Imperial Palace, 3535 Las Vegas Blvd. S. 702-794-3174. www.autocollections.com. Open year-round daily 9:30am–9:30pm. Free passes available online.

You've got wheels—lots of them – at the Imperial Palace Auto Collection. Regarded as one of the finest collections of its kind in the world, the exhibit showcases more than 750 antique, classic and special-interest vehicles spanning nearly 200 years of automotive history. Of these, more than 200 are on display—and for sale—at any one time in a gallery-like setting on the fifth floor of the Imperial Palace's parking structure.

The constantly rotating collection features vehicles once owned by famous people (James Cagney, Elvis Presley, Al Capone, Benito Mussolini). The collection also displays the rarest and some of the most exclusive and historically significant cars ever produced, including the world's largest collection of Model J Duesenbergs.

Holy Car!

The **1934 Ford V8 car★** of Bonnie and Clyde is on display at Terrible's Primm Valley Resort & Casino just outside of Las Vegas. The ghostly relic bears the scars of some 167 bullets fired in an ambush shoot-out with the law outside a remote Louisiana parish after the couple had managed to kill more than two dozen others. The car was sold to Primm for $250,000 and remains a popular and free attraction.

MUSEUMS

★Madame Tussauds Las Vegas

At The Venetian,
3377 Las Vegas Blvd. S.
702-862-7800. www.madametus
sauds.com/lasvegas. Open year-
round daily 10am–10pm (last
tickets sold 10pm). $25.

What do Tom Jones, Wayne Newton, Engelbert Humperdinck, Mick Jagger, Oprah Winfrey, George Clooney, Brad Pitt and more than 100 other celebrities have in common? They all have what it takes to get their likeness in Madame Tussaud's Las Vegas at the Venetian. When it comes to the making of a star, Madame Tussaud's has broken the mold. In this case, spinning off 105 to 110 masterfully crafted molds. Here you'll find realistic wax figures of some of the world's most popular film, television, music and sports celebrities, as well as legendary Las Vegas icons. They're all showcased at the Venetian's special two-story Las Vegas site. At Madame Tussaud's,

Astronauts and presidents share the stage

you can have your picture taken with your favorite stars—even marry them, sort of—just don't expect them to be animated about it. As unbelievably lifelike as they look, the only thing real about the figures is the clothing (most of the celebrities donated the garb that is presented).

New figures include Hugh Hefner, Cameron Diaz and the Blue Man Group. A Las Vegas exclusive is Evel Knievel in his prime in the mid '70s in his red, white and blue jumper and trademark cane. You can even sit on an authentic replica of one of his bikes—a 1972 Harley Davidson XR750, put on a themed Evel cape, and have your photo taken with the bike and Evel's life-like figure. A looping video of the dare-devil's feats—and

THE EXPERIENCE – Madame Tussauds allows you to live out your fantasy, whether that means marrying George Clooney (or marrying your honey but having George as your best man), singing with Britney, rocking with Elvis or playing with Shaquille. The museum is billed as an interactive "must-feel" attraction, and it's a "must- photograph" opportunity as well.

Johnny Depp, Madame Tussauds

crashes—plays in the background. Putt with Tiger, size up with Shaq. They're all here.

★Nevada State Museum and Historical Society

700 Twin Lakes Dr. 702-486-5205. www.nevadaculture.org. Open year-round daily 9am–5pm. Closed Jan 1, Thanksgiving Day & Dec 25. $4.

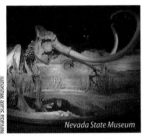

Nevada State Museum

This museum's story is Nevada's history, and this nationally accredited institution tells it with authority—from the wanderings of a 225-million-year-old ichthyosaur in the Mojave Desert to tourists prowling modern-day Las Vegas. Located in a pretty park with a duck pond, not far from downtown Las Vegas, the Nevada State Museum's permanent exhibits focus on the natural and anthropological history of the region.

Don't miss the recorded story of "Bugsy" Siegel's Flamingo Hotel, complete with his threats on his business partners' lives. The museum is one of several in Nevada, including a new one under construction in Springs Preserve.

The Liberace Museum

1775 E. Tropicana Ave. 702-798-5595. www.liberace.org/ liberacemuseum. Open Tue–Sat 10am–5pm, Sun noon–4pm. Closed Jan 1, Thanksgiving & Dec 25. $15.

Born Walter Valentino Liberace in West Allis, Wisconsin, the acclaimed pianist who came to be known as Liberace (1919–1986) first displayed his exceptional talent at the piano at age four. As a young man in the 1940s, Liberace played piano in a variety of night clubs. By 1952, Liberace had his own TV show, which won an Emmy for best entertainment program. Two years later, Liberace was earning $2 million for one

Liberace Museum

Joseph Augello

26-week season, making him the highest-paid pianist in the world. Liberace was known for his flash, which lives on in this museum (founded by the entertainer in 1979). Here Liberace's dazzling jewelry, unsurpassed wardrobe, custom car collection, and unique pianos—like the rhinestone-covered Baldwin that he played at his last performance at Radio City Music Hall—recall the artist's larger-than-life persona.

Add to the mix Liberace's glitzy 50-pound, 115,000-carat Austrian rhinestone—the biggest in the world (given to him as a gift by Swarovski and Company)—and you have a lot of bling-bling. But beyond the bling are some interesting artifacts.

Find an antique Louis XV desk from Russia's Czar Nicholas II, as well as examples of Liberace's Moser crystal among the baubles.

Las Vegas Art Museum

9600 W. Sahara Ave. 702-360-8000. www.lasvegasartmuseum.org. Open year-round, Tue–Sat 10am–5pm, Sun 1pm–5pm. $7.

By bringing ambitious fine art exhibitions to the community and the city's visitors, the Las Vegas Art Museum, now a Smithsonian affiliate, has further defined the evolving cultural landscape of Las Vegas. What was founded as a community art league in 1950 by dedicated volunteers, has turned into a respected art institution. The exhibition program features internationally recognized artists in all media and time periods. Past exhibitions have featured the work of Chagall, Dalí, Rodin, and contemporary glass artist Dale Chihuly. The museum's small but growing permanent collection includes works by Alexander Calder, Robert Indiana, Larry Rivers and Edward Ruscha.

The Springs Preserve

333 S. Valley View Blvd., 702-822-7700. www.springspreserve.org. Open daily 10am–10pm summer, until 6pm winter. $18.95.

Las Vegas' newest museum, the Springs Preserve is a $250 million non-gaming cultural attraction located a few miles west of The Strip with 180 acres of museums, botanical gardens, galleries, trails and entertainment elements.

An uncommon blend of interactive and educational experiences for all ages are folded into the visitor experience, which includes: an up-close look at a living bat cave, a brush with a live flash flood, a historic trail walk that passes by a Cienega (desert wetland), or an outdoor cooking demonstration in the botanical gardens. Children can climb aboard a 50-foot rattlesnake replica in the children's playground, visit the Preserve's resource library, master one of the many educational video games in the New Frontier Gallery or trade in their own artifacts at the Nature Exchange for other desired items. Families can cap their day with a live outdoor concert in the Springs Amphitheater, a light dinner in the Springs Café (operated by Wolfgang Puck) overlooking the Las Vegas Strip, and a stroll through the Canary Project photo gallery. And while browsing, visitors need not be concerned about leaving behind their dirty carbon footprints. The structures join an elite list of buildings nationwide for "Platinum" Leadership in Energy and Environmental Design (LEED) certification from the US Green Building Council (USGBC).

Las Vegas Natural History Museum

900 Las Vegas Blvd. N.
702-384-3466. www.lvnhm.org.
Open year-round daily 9am–4pm.
Closed Thanksgiving & Dec 25. $8.

Looking for ancient sharks or dinosaurs? The Las Vegas Natural History Museum's (LVNHM) multisensory exhibits are a good way to combine education and fun for all ages. Animated exhibits, robot dinosaurs (including a 35-foot-long *Tyrannosaurus rex*), live

fish and more than 26 species of preserved animals—including rare African water chevrotains (a cross between a pig and a deer), as well as zebra duikers from Liberia – take you from the neon jungle to the real jungle in a flash. There are even several "hands-on" areas where animals can be petted.

Las Vegas Gambling Museum

500 S. Main St. 702-385-7424.

Las Vegas is a museum in its own right, a quirky collection of neon, glass and water in fantasy-focused, made-to-be-imploded structures all in an improbable spot out in the middle of nowhere. And it collects its collectors, residents with their own ideas of what is valuable and interesting. All a visitor needs to do is walk along Main Street between Stratosphere and Downtown for a living museum of antiques and Vegas lore.
The best spot for this might be Main Street Antiques. The owner once operated the Las Vegas Gambling Museum inside the Tropicana Hotel and moved the entire collection to this site. Find rooms full of Las Vegas memorabilia on display in these cavernous quarters, from chips of long-gone casinos, to famous showgirl garb worn in legendary revues to vintage neon cocktail signs—and all of it is for sale. There's even an engaging historical exhibit on the mafia presence in Sin City. Bargaining is on the table here even if the chips are under glass. The store lies on the edge of the Las Vegas Arts District of studios and galleries and antique depots.

HISTORIC SITES

There were several phases of Las Vegas' Old West history—indeed, a couple of them notable for what happened clear out of town, in places like Boulder City and Overton. From the Wild West days to the era of large-scale local public waterworks like Hoover Dam, Vegas' colorful past comes alive at these sites.

★Bonnie Springs/ Old Nevada

1 Gunfighter Lane, Blue Diamond, NV. From The Strip, take Charleston Blvd. west for 25mi. 702-875-4191. www.bonniesprings.com. Shuttles are available from The Strip (call Star Land Tours; 702-296-4381). Open daily May–Sept 10:30am–6pm, Oct–Apr 10:30am–5pm. $20/car includes a $10 coupon for the ranchhouse restaurant.

The Wild West comes alive at Old Nevada, an 1880s mining town re-created on 115-acre Bonnie Springs Ranch. Nestled in Red Rock Canyon, a 30-minute drive from the Las Vegas Strip, Old Nevada provides plenty of rough-and-tumble action, including gunfights in the streets. There's also a miniature train ride, a wax museum illustrating figures from Nevada's frontier history,

a lovely 19C chapel, a restaurant, and shopping for turquoise, silver and Western souvenirs. The petting zoo, which houses deer, goats, raccoons, swans, llamas, and even a long-horned steer from Texas, is the most popular attraction on the property. On weekends, stay around for the posse show, an 1830s melodrama in which even the kids can help track down a mustachioed villain in an authentically recreated saloon. Of course, there's an obligatory public hanging with an obliging stunt-man who drops haplessly from the gallows and sways in the wind. The Ranch offers 🐴**horseback riding** with walking rides into the desert scrub. A fun thing to do here is have a hot drink on a cold day around the fire pit in the restaurant. This is a no-nonsense cowboy joint and serves great burgers. *No ties allowed.*

Boulder Theatre

★Boulder City

23mi southeast of Las Vegas via I-93/95 North or I-515 North.
702-293-2034.
www.bouldercity.com.

This charming little dry town (no alcohol) is the only city in Nevada that doesn't allow gaming. It was built by the government as a model city, and it has thrived on small-town values that are still very much in evidence today. Boulder City came into existence circa 1929 to house the workers constructing Hoover Dam and their families. Initially, there was some contention over where the dam was to be built—at Boulder Canyon or at Black Canyon (the latter won). Because the Boulder Canyon Project Act had been passed before the location was changed, all plans referred to the Boulder Dam project. That's why, when the Bureau of Reclamation commissioner, Dr. Elwood Mead, personally chose the townsite, he decided to call it Boulder City. From its vantage point overlooking Lake Mead, Boulder City makes a great base for enjoying all the recreational activities the lake provides. The city sits just around the corner *(7mi west)* from Hoover Dam. While you're here, relax in the central historic hotel plaza, browse through antique shops or grab a bite at the 1950s-style Coffee Cup Café.

Boulder's Grand Dame

Boris Karloff resided there; Bette Davis vacationed there; and Howard Hughes recuperated there after his plane crashed into Lake Mead. Will Rogers called the hotel home in 1935 when he performed at the Boulder Theatre. Built in 1933 to house government and corporate project managers overseeing the building of Hoover Dam, the Dutch Colonial-style **Boulder Dam Hotel** *(1305 Arizona St., Boulder City; 702-293-3510; www.boulderdamhotel.com)* is newly restored to its former glory after an eight-year renovation. Now a B&B, the 22-room lodging was placed on the National Register of Historic Places in 1982. Find a hidden museum of the Dam and the town here in the basement.

HISTORIC SITES

83

What's Left of the Fort?

- **Old Fort** (1855) – The adobe building closest to the creek is the only original part of the Mormons' 150-square-foot adobe fort, which featured towers and bastions on the northwest and southeast corners.
- **Ranch House** (1865) – Octavious Gass built this ranch house using part of the Old Fort's foundation.
- **Las Vegas Springs and Creek** – Running through the ranch site is a re-creation of the creek that supplied water to the area. After Las Vegas was founded, the water was diverted there, and the creek dried up.

Old Las Vegas Mormon State Historic Park

Nevada Division of State Parks

★Old Las Vegas Mormon State Historic Park

500 E. Washington Ave. at Las Vegas Blvd. 702-486-3511. www.parks.nv.gov/olvmf.htm. Open year-round daily 8am–4:30pm. $2.

This site was where Las Vegas began—the first permanent non-native settlement in the Las Vegas Valley. An adobe fort was built along Las Vegas Creek in 1855 by William Bringhurst and 29 of his fellow Mormons, who arrived here from Utah. The outpost, equipped with a post office, served as a way station for travelers along the Spanish Trail to California. The Mormons tried farming by diverting water from the creek, and even briefly dabbled in mining and smelting after lead was discovered in the mountains nearby. But after two years, with internal conflicts and Indian raids, the Mormons abandoned the fort. In 1865, Octavious D. Gass, a miner from El Dorado Canyon, bought the land and established a small store and blacksmith shop on-site. Gass defaulted on a note in 1881 and the ranch house was taken over by Archibald and Helen Stewart. After Archibald was killed in a gunfight in 1884, Helen and her father continued to operate the ranch. In 1902 Helen sold the place along with the water rights to the San Pedro, Los Angeles & Salt Lake Railroad, which chugged into the valley in 1905. The fort was eventually renovated in 1929.

Old Las Vegas Mormon State Historic Park

Nevada Division of State Parks

★Spring Mountain Ranch State Park

16mi west of Las Vegas via Charleston Blvd. 702-875-4141. www.parks.nv.gov/smr.htm. Open year-round daily 8am–dusk; main ranch house 10am–4pm. $5.

This 520-acre ranch is located at 3,800 feet, at the base of the Wilson Cliffs in the Red Rock Canyon National Conservation Area. In the first half of the 19C, pack and wagon trains used this site, with its spring-fed creek and tranquil meadows, as a campsite and watering hole, as they headed west along the Spanish Trail. James Wilson, an army sergeant based at Fort Mohave, and his partner, George Anderson, lay claim to the property in 1876 and named it Sand Stone Ranch. After surviving a long string of owners—including Howard Hughes—the ranch became a state park in 1971.

The picturesque red main **ranch house** now serves as a visitor center. Visitors are encouraged to acquaint themselves with the area and then take a self-guided tour through the interior of the ranch house.

A guided tour of the historic area includes the two second-oldest buildings in the Las Vegas Valley: an early 19C blacksmith shop and a sandstone cabin. You'll also see the reservoir created in 1945 by former owner and radio personality Chet Lauck (dubbed Lake Harriet, for his wife), as well as the gravesites of the Wilson family, who originally homesteaded the property. Periodic living-history demonstrations interpret life on the frontier.

Blue Diamond

Junction of Hwy 159 and Hwy 160. 25 miles southwest of Las Vegas.

Just down the road from Bonnie Springs and Spring Mountain Ranch is Blue Diamond, a quiet hamlet shaded by cottonwoods permanently lodged in the 1950s. About 300 people live there, read at the library and shop at the spot's only store. It's a true getaway's getaway.

All is quiet here, but for the occasional sound of a barking dog or braying mule. Created in the '40s for the workers of the nearby gypsum mine it's now a cool artifact of a time long gone.

Spring Mountains Ranch State Park

Las Vegas news bureau/LVCVA

NATURAL SITES

Leaving Las Vegas for a day trip into its scenic environs can provide more than just a getaway from the action of the city. It can offer a quiet foray into some of the most interesting geological formations of the Old West.

Red Rock Canyon

Red Rock Canyon NCA

★★Red Rock Canyon

Red Rock Canyon is 23mi west of Las Vegas via W. Charleston Blvd. (Rte. 159). Look for the sign on the right to Red Rock Scenic Drive. Red Rock Visitor Center is located at 1000 Scenic Dr. 702-363-1921. www.redrockcanyonlv.org. Hours vary seasonally. $5/car.

A 40-minute drive from the Las Vegas Strip, the towering sandstone bluffs of Red Rock Canyon are magnificent to a fault—the Keystone Thrust Fault, to be exact, the most significant geologic feature of the canyon. Scientists think that some 65 million years ago, two of the earth's crustal

Riding The Range

Horses can be rented through **Red Rock Riding Stables** or Red Rock Resort *(702-797-7777; 866-767-7773)*. Reserve a spot on the two-hour sunset trail ride through the canyons, which culminates with a campfire dinner.

plates collided with such force that part of one plate was shoved up and over younger sandstone through this fracture in the earth's crust. Dazzling formations abound in this park carved from sand dunes cemented and tinted by water acting on iron oxide and calcium carbonate then amassing in magnificent swirls. With more than 30 miles of trails, the 300-square-mile **Red Rock Canyon National Conservation Area★★** preserves the northern end of these geologic events. The area's **Red Rock Visitor Center★** is the place to get all the information you need. A recorded tour recounts the area's ancient and natural history. From the visitors center, you can drive the 13-mile Scenic Loop, open from 7am to dusk with panoramic views of spectacular rock formations. Highlights include **sandstone quarry★**, a 2.5 mile hike up **Ice-Box Canyon★**, and **Willow Spring**, with its ancient petroglyphs. Find picnic tables, maps and toilets at the trailheads.

MUST SEE

Self-Guided Driving Tour Highlights

Mouse's Tank★★ – The intriguing -**Petroglyph Canyon Trail★★** (.8mi) crosses a narrow canyon to Mouse's Tank. Named for a Paiute Indian who hid from the law here in 1897, this natural rock basin collects rainwater and provides a watering spot for birds, reptiles, mammals and insects.

White Domes Area★★ – From the visitor center, a 7-mile spur road leads to the White Domes, a landscape of mulitcolored monuments and smooth, wind-carved sandstone.

Atlatl Rock★ – On the west end of the park, a steep metal stairway climbs up to Atlatl Rock, where you'll find a rare petroglyph of an atlatl, a notched stick used to throw primitive spears.

★★Valley of Fire State Park

48mi northeast of Las Vegas via I-15 North to Hwy. 169. Visitor center is located on Rte. 169 in Overton, NV. 702-397-2088. http://parks.nv.gov/vf.htm. Visitor center open year-round daily 8:30am–4:30pm. Nominal fees posted at entrance.

You may think you're on Mars when you first gaze upon the jagged limestone mounds of fiery scarlet, vermillion and mauve that rise out of the stark Mojave Desert. The 56,000-acre park, dedicated in 1935 as Nevada's first state park, takes its name from its distinctive coloration. The red sandstone formations that make up this surreal scene were formed from great sand dunes during the Jurassic Period. Complex uplifting and faulting in the region, followed by 100 million years of erosion, have carved this 6-mile-long and 4-mile-wide crimson-hued valley from the desert. In the process, water and wind have shaped the land into arches, domes, spires and serrated ridges.

Valley of Fire is famous for its **petroglyphs**—ancient rock art left behind by the prehistoric Basketmaker people and the Anasazi Pueblo farmers who lived along the Muddy River between 300 BC and AD 1150.

It's wise to stop at the visitor center before exploring the area. There you can pick up maps, trail guides and books, and learn about the ecology, geology and history of the region. A drive through the valley takes about 20 minutes.

Valley of Fire State Park

beehives
Once part of a sand deposit that covered a vast area, these rocks have been subjected to a relentless attack by harsh winds, rain, heat and cold, creating the many unusual formations that make up the Valley of Fire.

Las Vegas News Bureau/ LVCVA

NATURAL SITES

Tips for Visiting

The best time to visit the preserve is in spring or autumn. Temperatures between mid-May and mid-September soar upwards from 100°F. The 67-mile circuit from Baker via Kelbaker Road, Kelso-Cima Road and Cima Road to I-15 is a good introduction to the park's sights.

★Mojave National Preserve

53mi south of Las Vegas via I-15, in Baker, CA; alternate entry 113mi south of Furnace Creek via I-15 to Rte. 127. Contact the Kelso Depot Information Center (760-252-6108).
Open year-round daily 9am–5pm. www.nps.gov/moja. Park HQ at 2701 Barstow Rd., Barstow, CA. 760-252-6100.

If you're wondering just how vast and empty the desert can be, the Mojave National Preserve is the answer to your question.
An easy day trip from Las Vegas, the 1.6 million-acre preserve (which begins near Baker, California) is crisscrossed by both paved and dirt roads.
The Mojave is home to nearly 300 animal species and some 700 plant species, including the nation's largest Joshua forest.
The 2,500-square-mile wedge-shaped preserve encompasses a landscape of lava mesas, precipitous mountain ranges, sand dunes, limestone caverns, dry lake beds and lava tubes.
Although mines and ranches still operate in the area (watch for "no trespassing" signs), evidence of human habitation is rare. Livestock graze safely thanks to the California Desert Protection Act, and hunting is allowed, although half the preserve is designated as wilderness.
The best time to visit is March through April when carpets of wildflowers blanket the hills and canyons. But stay on trails to avoid snakes as the weather warms.

Joshua tree in Mojave National Preserve

©Andrea Hornackova/Dreamstime.com

Mojave Highlights

Hole-in-the-Wall★★ – This jumble of volcanic cliffs, one of the more bizarre geologic features of Black Canyon, is profusely pocked with clefts and cavities.
Kelso Dunes★ – The 45 acres of Kelso Dunes are among the highest in the Mojave (600 feet above the desert floor).
Mitchell Caverns★ – Six limestone caverns are concealed within the Providence Mountains, which were formed by percolating groundwater millions of years ago.

★Spring Mountains National Recreation Area

35mi northwest of downtown Las Vegas. From The Strip, take I-15 West to Hwy. 95 North. Stay on Hwy. 95 until you get to Kyle Canyon Rd. and follow signs for Mt. Charleston. U.S. Forest Service oversees the park: 702-515-5400. www.fs.fed.us/r4/htnf/districts/smnra. Call for campground information.

If you're pining for a beautiful alpine wilderness spot to get away from it all, **Mt. Charleston** and the surrounding Humboldt-Toiyabe National Forest is a popular destination for 🥾**activities** like hiking, backpacking, picnicking and overnight camping.

Thick bristlecone pines (among the oldest trees on earth), clinging to the limestone cliffs 10,000 feet above the desert floor, make for an awesome backdrop.

The fifth-highest mountain in the state, at just under 12,000 feet, Mt. Charleston experiences temperatures that are usually anywhere from 20 to 40 degrees cooler than Las Vegas (rarely going above 80 degrees in the summer). You'll notice the change in vegetation with each incremental increase in elevation. Besides the distinctive plant life, many animals inhabit the Mt. Charleston area. Among them is the Palmer chipmunk, which is found nowhere else in the world. The region is also home to bighorn sheep, elk, coyotes, bobcats, foxes and cougars. The U.S. Forest Service maintains more than 50 miles of marked hiking trails for all abilities at Mt. Charleston. The most challenging hike is the 8.3-mile **South Loop Trail**, which climbs to the mountain's 11,918-foot summit from the head of Kyle Canyon Road.

In winter there is skiing at Lee Canyon, just down the road from Mt. Charleston Lodge at the end of Hwy 156 *(702–385-2754; www. skilasvegas.com)*.

Las Vegas News Bureau/LVCVA

Spring Mountains National Recreation Area

NATURAL SITES

EXCURSIONS

You won't want to miss the boat when it comes to two of the Las Vegas area's most popular day trips, Lake Mead and Hoover Dam. If you're willing to venture a bit farther afield, within a day's drive of Las Vegas, the natural wonders of the Grand Canyon, the Mojave Desert and the Red Rock country of Sedona, Arizona await you.

★★★Hoover Dam

*31mi southeast of Las Vegas
via US-93 South. 702-294-3523.
www.usbr.gov/lc/hooverdam.
Open year-round daily 9am–6pm.
Closed Thanksgiving & Dec 25.
Parking $7; adult tickets $11.*

One of the more impressive views in the region, this engineering wonder of the modern world supplies water for more than 25 million people. Hoover Dam was built against all odds as a WPA project during the Depression and claimed more than 100 lives in the process. Conditions were harsh, heat was horrible, wages disappeared in the nearby brothels and casinos. In 1935, the flood gates

Voices of the Damed

Some 16,000 men and women worked on the dam during its 13 years of construction. And 112 lost their lives from it, including J.G. Tierney who drowned while surveying and was the first fatality. His son Patrick died 13 years later to the day and was the dam's last fatality. It is said if you listen closely enough you can hear ghosts in the tunnels.

opened and the mighty Colorado River backed up into what is now Lake Mead.

A tour of the dam is a self-guided experience that includes films, murals, exhibits, talks by knowledgeable staff in various locations, and the chance to take elevators down to the bottom of the dam, walk through a 250-ft tunnel drilled through the bedrock, and view the 650-ft Nevada wing of the power plant and its eight huge generators. Four huge 30-foot-diameter pipes transport nearly 90,000 gallons of water each second from Lake Mead to the hydroelectric generators in the powerhouse. It takes two hours to see all there is to see at Hoover Dam during the day, but you can see a different side of the dam if you come late at night. Phosphorescent floodlights cast an eerie glow down concrete walls as the lazy Colorado flows through to Black Canyon.

Hoover Dam

Las Vegas News Bureau/LVCVA

MUST SEE

★★★Grand Canyon National Park

The two main access points, the South Rim and the North Rim, are 214mi apart by road. Most visitor activities in the park are located on the South Rim. To reach the South Rim, take US-93 South through Boulder City to Kingman, AZ, about 90mi; exit on Hwy. 40 East to Williams, and drive north on Hwys. 64 & 180 to Grand Canyon Village. To get to the North Rim (open mid-May–mid-Oct; reservations advised), take I-15 North to Hwy. 9 South; go south on Hwy. 89 at Mt. Carmel junction. South Rim is 260mi east of Las Vegas in Arizona. The North Rim is 275mi east of Las Vegas. 928-638-7888. www.nps. gov/grca. Open year-round daily 24 hours. $25/car for a 7-day pass; $12 no car.

Located in northwest Arizona, this 1,904 sq mi national park is a designated World Heritage Site. The canyon was carved over the eons by the Colorado River, and today a giant swath of the earth's geological history appears in the colorful striated layers of rock, which reach down more than a mile below the canyon's rim. At dawn and dusk, when the low-angle sun lights the vividly colored canyon walls, the 277-mile-long Grand Canyon is an awesome and humbling sight.

★★★SOUTH RIM

Grand Canyon Village – Site of the park headquarters, the main visitor center and the lion's share of hotels and restaurants and tourist facilities, this area includes the **Grand Canyon Village★** Historical District. Free shuttle bus.

★★★East Rim Drive – The 24-mile road from Grand Canyon Village to the East Rim Entrance Station passes numerous dizzying viewpoints.

★★West Rim Skywalk – Visitors to the western rim of the Grand Canyon can walk out beyond the precipice and see nothing but thin air all the way down to the Colorado River nearly a mile below via the Skywalk that opened in March 2007. The Skywalk is the first-ever cantilever-shaped glass walkway to suspend more than 4,000ft above the canyon's floor and extend 70ft from the canyon's rim. *Reservations required. www. grandcanyonskywalk.com or www. destinationgrandcanyon.com.*

©National Park Service

Grand Canyon viewed from Pima Point on the West Rim Drive

★★NORTH RIM

Open mid-May–mid-Oct, weather permitting.

Less developed and more remote than the South Rim, the North Rim is also more spectacular, set in the deep forest of the Kaibab Plateau. **Bright Angel Point** – From the visitor center adjacent to Grand Canyon Lodge, a paved half-mile trail ends at Bright Angel Point with glorious **views★★★** of the canyon.

★Cape Royal Road – This road extends 23 miles from Grand Canyon Lodge southeast across the Walhalla Plateau to Cape Royal. A spur route leads to Point Imperial, the highest spot on the canyon rim at 8,803 feet.

From north to south the canyon spans some 215 miles and will take about five hours to drive.

Most visitors head to the South Rim of the park as it is open all year and features the most attractions. A \$25 seven-day pass to drive through the park will be required. Consider parking at Grand Canyon Village (free in most spots) and taking a hop-on-hop-off tram to

No Yawns Here

A five-and-a-half-hour drive from Las Vegas, the canyon is best visited in April, May and September, when the summer crowds have left. The 7,000-foot elevation keeps the South Rim from becoming unbearably hot in the summer; however the canyon bottom can reach temperatures of 110°F. From December to March, the upper canyon is usually snowbound. If you have more time, you can take a mule trip *(reserve several months in advance)*, or hike to the bottom of the canyon.

such popular spots as the historic El Tovar Hotel, Hopi House, Kolb Studio gallery and Yavapai Observation Station, all interspersed with plenty of look-outs, mini-museums, gift shops, and refreshment outlets. A National Geographic IMAX movie is worth the watch, in its location just outside the park in the village of Tusayan, South Rim. Or head to the airport there for a 30-minute helicopter ride of your life.

Grand Canyon

©Ryan Morgan/iStockphoto.com

How the Grand Canyon Was Formed

In the earth's infancy, the area now defined by the Grand Canyon was covered by shallow coastal waters and active volcanoes. Over millions of years, layers of marine sediment and lava built to depths thousands of feet thick. About 1.7 billion years ago, heat and pressure from within the earth buckled the sedimentary layers into mountains 5–6mi high, changing their composition to a metamorphic rock called Vishnu schist. Molten intrusions in the mountains' core cooled and hardened into pink granite, then eroded. The process repeated itself: another shallow sea covering the land, more layers of sediment—12,000ft thick now. A new mountain range formed and eroded and the ancient Vishnu schist was laid bare.

The horizontal layers above the schist, to 3,500ft below the modern canyon rim, were formed over 300 million years as oceans advanced across the Southwest and then regressed. The environment was alternately marsh and desert as dinosaurs roamed. Then the Colorado River began to cut the canyon about 65 million years ago, gouging through rock and carrying the debris to sea. As erosion thinned the layer of rock above the earth's core, lava spewed to the surface. In fact, there have been several periods of recent volcanic activity in the Grand Canyon area, most recently in the 11C at Sunset Crater, southeast of the park.

GEOLOGIC LAYERS OF THE GRAND CANYON

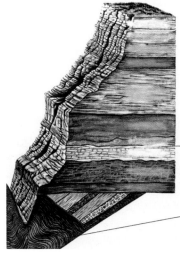

Kaibab Formation

Toroweap Formation

Coconino Sandstone

Hermit Shale

Supai Group

Redwall Limestone

Temple Butte Formation
Muav Limestone

Bright Angel Shale

Tapeats Sandstone

Precambrian Rocks of
the Inner Gorge

EXCURSIONS

★★★Death Valley National Park

120mi west of Las Vegas via I-15 South and Hwy. 160. Go through Pahrump and take State Line Rd. to Death Valley Junction; at the junction, take Hwy. 190 to the park. Death Valley Visitor Center is located on Hwy. 190 at Furnace Creek. 760-786-3200. www.nps.gov/deva. Open year-round daily 8am–5pm. $10.

At first glance this infamous valley seems to be appropriately named, but in fact only one pioneer is known to have died trying to cross it. When you stand in this vast, silent, stark landscape, it does indeed seems inescapable.

An enormous basin (130 miles long and 5 to 25 miles wide), the valley formed progressively as a block of the earth's crust sagged and sank between parallel mountain ranges, creating an astounding difference in elevation. Altitudes range from 282 feet below sea level at Badwater to 11,049 feet at Telescope Peak.

Designated as a national park under the 1994 Desert Protection Act, Death Valley is now the largest national park outside Alaska, covering more than 3.3 million acres. This is one of the hottest and driest places on earth: Annual precipitation averages less than two inches, and the highest temperature ever recorded in the US—134°F at Furnace Creek in 1913—has been exceeded only in the Sahara Desert.

Zabrieskie Point, Death Valley National Park

©PhotoDisc

Furnace Creek Inn & Resort

Hwy. 190 in Death Valley National Park. 760-786-2345. www.furnacecreekresort. com. 66 inn rooms; 224 ranch rooms. $250–$400, inn; $105–$192, ranch.

There's no need to rough it in the desert when you can stay at the Furnace Creek Inn. The inn and adjacent Furnace Creek Ranch have served as a welcoming oasis for visitors since the 1930s. You'll find everything you could ask for here— renovated air-conditioned rooms with ceiling fans, a restaurant, a spring-fed swimming pool, tennis courts, and an 18-hole golf course. The general store stocks camping supplies, but why would you want to leave this lovely place?

BEST OF DEATH VALLEY

★Badwater Road – *Rte. 178, south of Furnace Creek.*
This 36-mile road follows Death Valley's descent to the lowest point in the Americas.

★★Zabriskie Point – *Rte. 190, 4.5mi east of Furnace Creek.*
This renowned point commands splendid views over Golden Canyon.

★★★Dante's View – *24mi southeast of Furnace Creek via Rte. 190 to Dante's View Rd.*
From a 5,475-foot perch atop the Amargosa Range, this stunning **view★★★** takes in the continent's most extreme elevation change.

★★Stovepipe Wells Sand Dunes – *6mi east of Stovepipe Wells on Rte. 190.*
The park's most accessible sand dunes pile up in billowing hills.

★Scotty's Castle – *53mi north of Furnace Creek on Rte. 267.*
This lavish Spanish-Moorish mansion, built in 1924 as a winter retreat for Chicago millionaire Albert Johnson, is named after Johnson's flamboyant friend, Walter Scott, also known as "Death Valley Scotty."

★★Sedona

276mi southeast of Las Vegas in Arizona. Take US-93 South to I-40 East to US-89A South. Visitor information: 928-282-7722 or www.sedonachamber.com.

This small city in northern Arizona owes its beauty and mystique to the staggering variety of striking red buttes and spires that surround it. Sedona's red rocks have been a beacon for those seeking spiritual enlightenment since the 1980s, when some of its sites (Cathedral Rock, Bell Rock, Boynton Canyon) were found to emit concentrated electromagnetic energy.

Located in the heart of Arizona's **Red Rock Country★★★**, Sedona is bounded by Oak Creek and Sycamore canyons, the Mogollon Rim and Verde Valley. The region takes its name from the rust color exposed in three mid-level strata of the Supai Group, the Hermit Formation and the Schnebly Hill Formation, all sculpted of sandstone between 270 to 300 million years ago.

Sedona's commercial area, north of the "Y" intersection of US-89A, teems with Native American craft shops and New Age boutiques. When the town gets too touristy,

Red Rocks of Sedona

©Nick Martucci/iStockphoto.com

you're just a short drive—by off-road vehicle—away from Red Rock Country. Several companies offer off-road jeep tours, but if you're driving yourself, **Schnebly Hill Road** provides the most convenient backcountry access. The 12-mile route turns from pavement to rutted dirt after the first mile, but if you press onward, you'll be rewarded by dazzling views of red rock formations and a panorama of the valley below. In the heat of summer try slipping and sliding down the natural rockslide in Oak Creek Canyon, just outside of town. Or go hunting for vortexes, areas in the earth where the magnetic forces converge to create energy pockets—or so they say. Sedona is reputed to be rife with such spots.

★Lake Mead National Recreation Area

27mi south of Las Vegas via US-93 at the junction of Lakeshore Scenic Dr. (Rte. 166). 702-293-8990. www.nps.gov/lame. Visitor center open year-round daily 8:30am–4:30pm. $5.

Embracing two vast reservoirs on the Colorado River, this 2,350 sq mi desert preserve was created in 1936 when the natural flow of the Colorado River was blocked by Hoover Dam. The largest man-

Rooms With A View

★**Montezuma Castle National Monument** – *5mi south of Sedona in Camp Verde. Take I-17 South to Exit 289 and follow signs. 928-567-3322. www.nps.gov/moca. Open year-round daily 8am–5pm (until 6pm in summer). $3.*
Impossibly tucked into a natural limestone alcove 50 to 100 feet above the floor of Beaver Creek, Montezuma Castle was part of a 12C Sinaguan community.
★**Tuzigoot National Monument** – *23mi southwest of Sedona; off Rte. 279 in Clarksville, AZ. 928-634-5564. www.nps.gov/tuzi. Open daily 8am–5pm (until 7pm in summer). Closed Dec 25. $3.* This circa 1300 Sinagua pueblo rises 120 feet above the Verde River with 86 rooms to explore.

Smooth Sailing
Visit the **Alan Bible Visitor Center** *(Lakeshore Scenic Dr. at Rte. 93; 702-293-8990; www.nps.gov/archive/lame/visitorcenter)*, a few miles west of Hoover Dam to pick up information about recreational activities at the lake. Be sure to take a jaunt around the lake on the *Desert Princess*, a 100-foot-long triple-deck pad-dlewheeler that offers lunch, brunch, dinner, dancing, and even pizza cruises around the lake *(cruises depart from Lake Mead Marina near Boulder Beach; www. lakemeadcruises.com)*.

made lake in the US, Lake Mead can hold enough water to cover the entire state of Nevada with six inches of water. More than nine million visitors each year come here to boat, fish, water ski, swim, camp, picnic and explore. Lake Mead is the centerpiece of the Lake Mead Recreation Area, which also includes Lake Mojave to the south and the surrounding desert east and north. There are numerous sandy beaches, se-cluded coves and narrow canyons accessible only by water. With water temperatures averaging 78 degrees in spring, summer and autumn, the clear lake is ideal for swimming. A fun way to explore this lake is by houseboat rental and anchoring in remote coves.

Lost City Museum exhibit

Lost City Museum of Archeology

★Lost City Museum of Archeology

63mi northeast of Las Vegas. 721 S. Moapa Valley Blvd., Overton, NV. Take I-15 North to Hwy. 169 and follow Hwy. 169 through Overton. The museum is about 15mi past Overton on the right. 702-397-2193. www.comnett.net/ ~kolson. Open year-round daily 8:30am–4:30pm. Closed Jan 1, Thanksgiving Day & Dec 25. $3.

The Lost City refers to the Pueblo Grande de Nevada, a series of Anasazi ruins set along the Muddy and Virgin river valleys in southern Nevada. The entire Anasazi culture, which established itself in the valley beginning about 300 BC, mysteriously disappeared from the area between AD 1150 and AD 1250.
The museum was built on an Anasazi ruin and houses artifacts excavated from area Anasazi sites.

Lake Mead windsurfing

EXCURSIONS

97

THRILL RIDES

Your fun factor will accelerate from 0–60 in an instant when you experience Las Vegas' thrill rides. The Gs have it in places such as Stratosphere, New York-New York, Buffalo Bill's and the Sahara, where speed and height are the name of the game.

The Big Shot

At the Stratosphere Tower, Level 112. 2000 Las Vegas Blvd. S. 702-380-7777 or 800-998-6937. www.stratospherehotel.com. Open year-round Sun–Thu 10am–1am, Fri–Sat 10am–2am. Riders must be at least 52 inches tall. See Insanity–The Ride for prices.

Fun at 160ft – the Big Shot

Preferred Public Relations & Marketing

If you're looking for a real adrenaline rush, treat yourself to the Big Shot, one of the world's two highest thrill rides.

Only for the truly daring, the ride carries a total of 12 passengers at a time, launching them 160 feet in 2.5 seconds up the 238-foot mast that extends like a needle from the top of the Tower, the tallest open air point in the city. You'll experience four Gs of pressure on the way up; then you'll hang suspended for a split second before hitting zero-G weightlessness on the way down as you drop faster than normal free fall. If your eyes are closed tight, you'll miss a great view of the city.

Cyber Speedway at the Sahara

Sahara Hotel & Casino, 2535 S. Las Vegas Blvd. 702-737-2111 or 888-696-2121. www.saharalasvegas.com/ content/NASCAR/cyber-speedway. Open year-round Sun–Thu 10am–midnight (Fri & Sat until 1am). Riders must be 54 inches tall. $10 for Cyber Speedway or Speed–The Ride. An all-day pass for both cars and coaster is $21.95.

The Sahara took on a NASCAR theme during its last update and created a thrill ride based on a racing motif. The Cyber Speedway offers riders the chance to maneuver mock race cars around a virtual track chasing the checkered flag. Compete against yourself or challenge other drivers at virtual speeds of up to 220mph. Cars are mounted on hydraulic bases and are equipped with collision-detection capabilities on a six-axis motion system. It's as close to racing as you can get without venturing onto the real track.

Speed – The Ride

While you're at the Sahara, try some real gut-wrenching speed that will actually put wind in your face.

The linear-induction technology uses electromagnetic force to propel 24 riders at a time out of the hotel at speeds of 70mph down a 1,300-foot-long track and up a

Speed, The Ride

Lark Ellen Gould/MICHELIN

224-foot vertical rise, then drops them back down for a breath-defying reversed experience.

Insanity–The Ride

At the Stratosphere Tower, Level 112. 2000 Las Vegas Blvd. S. 702-380-7777. www.stratospherehotel.com. Open year-round Sun–Thu 10am–1am, Fri–Sat 10am–2am. Riders must be at least 48 inches tall. $12. Tower admission & a single ride is $19.95. Combination ticket for

X Scream, Insanity and Big Shot is $27.95; an all-day unlimited thrill-ride pass at Stratosphere costs $33.95.

As the tallest structure in Las Vegas (and west of the Mississippi River) at more than 1,149 feet, the Stratosphere Tower gives thrill-seekers a hearty dose of negative Gs on its new ride. Insanity is the latest in acrophobic-challenging rides at this resort, which holds all the honors for having the highest thrill rides in the world. Named for the state of mind riders must be in to climb onto a contraption that has been described as an inverted centrifuge, Insanity is a one-of-kind attraction.

On this ride, ten passengers board "escape-proof" seats and are spun at 40mph over the edge of the tower, with nothing shielding them from the city more than 900 feet below. A giant arm flings folks 64 feet over the edge of the tower, then spins them at a rate that induces up to three negative Gs. As the ride spins faster and faster, riders are propelled up to an angle of 70 degrees, until they are

Brian Jones

Insanity at the Stratosphere Hotel

literally facing downward, looking at the city below.

✈Air Combat USA

At N. Las Vegas Airport,
2730 Airport Drive, 800-522-7590.
www.aircombatusa.com. $1,395.

If speed doesn't get the adrenals working perhaps a few war games will. Air Combat USA hubs at North Las Vegas Airport and offers a pre-set schedule of Top Gun experiences over the Mojave Desert. The session does not require pilot training and allows the guest pilot to take control of the dogfight once the SIAI Marchetti SF260 Italian-built fighter aircraft is aloft and the "enemy" is in view.

The aircraft has a side-by-side seating arrangement, dual stick controls, 260 horsepower and flies at 270mph, in a range of +6 to -3 Gs for stomach-wrenching realism. Most of the instructors at the flight controls have served their time as military pilots and top secret pilot tips come with the tariff as do fitted flight suits and helmets, parachutes and instructions on how to use them. A dose of preparation in ground school covers the tactical maneuvers required to get results during a death-rattling dog fight and passengers are taken from armchair dreamer to air warrior in those moments for the ultimate adventure fantasy. Guests actually fly the airborne aircraft most of the session and take aim with electric bullets and an electronic tracking system. Direct hits register with sound effects and smoke trails. Three cockpit cameras record all the action for keepsake videos. The entire afternoon lasts around three hours. *Check for schedules.*

Manhattan Express

Las Vegas News Bureau/LVCVA

✈Manhattan Express Roller Coaster

At New York-New York,
3790 Las Vegas Blvd. S.
702-740-6969 or 888-693-6763.
www.nynyhotelcasino.com.
Open year-round Sun–Thu 11am–
11pm, Fri–Sat 10:30am–midnight.
$14/ride; $7.00/re-ride.

Around and around and around she goes, and where she stops, you'll definitely know. Just try to smile at the end of your Manhattan Express roller coaster ride (even if you're feeling pretty green); that's when the pictures are taken. The Manhattan Express twists, loops and dives at speeds up to 60mph delivering as much as 3.7 Gs (astronauts experience 3.2 Gs on launch) as the roller coaster winds around skyscrapers and the Statue of Liberty. At times, your whole world will literally turn upside down. This ride features the first-ever "heartline" twist-and-dive maneuver, which creates the sensation that a pilot feels when performing a barrel roll in an airplane. In this portion of the ride, the train rolls 180 degrees, suspending its riders 86 feet above the casino before diving directly under itself and into the hotel.

🎢 Las Vegas Motor Speedway

7000 Las Vegas Blvd N.
702-644-4444 or 800-644-4444
www.lvms.com.
The 1500-acre Las Vegas Motor Speedway complex includes a 1.5-mile superspeedway, 2.5-mile road course, .5-mile dirt oval and drag strip.

For adventure that truly puts pedal to the metal, Las Vegas is ground zero for auto racing. Most of the action can be found almost any day at Las Vegas Motor Speedway in North Las Vegas, a course of four different tracks used by major auto racing events including several NASCAR name-makers. The Las Vegas Metro police force trains on these tracks and so can visitors who feed on speed and want to quell their gasoline addiction. The **Richard Petty Driving Experience** *(800-237-3889;*

www.1800bepetty.com) straps in riders behind the wheel or in the shotgun seat of a custom-built stock car for as many as 40 laps around the 1.5-mile elliptical course at speeds of at least 150mph in the passenger seat. Packaged rates can include transfers from Strip hotels. Advanced Racing Experience packages for die hard fans can go as high as $2,599. Or, you can just go for the ride for $109.

Similarly, **Freddie Spencer's High Performance Riding School** *(888- 672-7219; www.fastfreddie. com)* puts all the action of Petty on two wheels. The three-time Grand Prix champion, Freddie Spencer, throws two- and three-day courses into the hands of thrill fans, custom-geared for any level of motorcycle enthusiast for costs ranging from $2,395 to $3,195. The champion bike racer helped to engineer the modern aerodynamics and machine precision Grand Prix race bikes use today. Students learn their moves on the latest Honda CBR600s, the legendary Honda CBR1000RR Fireblade, the Honda Interceptor or the Honda CRF100F. The price of the school

Las Vegas Motor Speedway

Las Vegas Motor Speedway

THRILL RIDES

includes equipment, transportation to and from the Orleans Hotel, breakfast, lunch and other extras, such as videotaped track sessions. Leather protective gear can be rented at the facility.

Indy-style racing fans hit the pavement at 145 to 180mph at the **Mario Andretti Racing School** *(877-263-7388; www.andrettiracing. com)*, which uses its own custom-built full-size single-seat cars, powered by 600-horsepower Chevy V8s with a single-speed gearbox. Participants can get the fastest go-kart ride of their life in three short laps with the **Champ Ride**, which for $99 offers a taste of true Indy-car racing. Options available run up to $5,000 for Fantasy Day driving three different race cars with Mario Andretti graduate certificate, printed lap times, souvenir racing license and insurance.

Zero Gravity

At McCarran Airport.
800-937-6480. www.gozerog.com.
$5,000 per person, including all taxes and fees.

Float above the neon in a reconfigured 737. The operative word here is FLOAT. Based in Las Vegas, Zero-G flights take place regularly with dates placed on the web site. It could possibly be the most frightening and most thrilling ride any one will ever have and that is because it takes a plane empty of seats and galleys, covers the windows and transports around two dozen people at top speed into the upper altitudes of commercial air space. Passengers start out by lying prone on the base of the plane and float upwards

as the plane dips and arcs in a series of parabolic maneuvers, ultimately mimicking the effects of weightlessness for the riders. Passengers get their fair share of 20 to 30-second floats during a three or four-hour flight. They float to piped-in music during dips and arcs through the atmosphere and take a champagne toast to their day upon landing. The experience is available out of McCarran International Airport and the costs include all the free logo gear they give you at the end. The company took physics professor and author Stephen Hawking for a test flight. The scientist, who is paralyzed from Lou Gehrig's Disease and is known for his contributions to the fields of cosmology and quantum gravity (especially in the context of black holes), was able to live out one of his dreams and float against the laws of gravity without constraint.

X Scream

At the Stratosphere Tower, Level 112. 2000 Las Vegas Blvd. S. 702-380-7777. www.stratospherehotel.com. Open year-round Sun–Thu 10am–1am, Fri–Sat 10am–2am. Riders must be at least 48 inches tall. See Insanity–The Ride for prices (p99).

The 60 seconds that you spend dangling over Las Vegas in the seats of X-Scream will seem like an eternity. Passengers are loaded into cars that are open to the elements, with only single lap bars to keep riders in their seats. Described as a high-tech teeter-totter, the ride operates on an 86-foot track that hoists riders high into the air before diving at a

30-degree angle, wrenching both nerves and stomachs. The arm of X Scream stretches out 27 feet over the edge of the Stratosphere Tower and, after reaching speeds of 30mph, jerks to a sudden stop, taking the scream right out of frozen throats and leaving riders 900 feet above the ground to contemplate life as they knew it.

SkyDive Las Vegas

1401 Airport Road, Boulder City, 702-SKY-DIVE (759-3483) or 800-U-SKYDIVE (875-9348). www.skydivelasvegas.com. $199.

Thrill junkies who prefer to fly without a plane can book an afternoon with Skydive Las Vegas, which specializes in first-time jumpers. Participants pay per skydive but can take all the pre-flight training they want with classes running daily at 8am, 10am , noon and 2pm by appointment. Flights take off from Boulder City Airport near the Hoover Dam and, from two miles above Boulder City, with a bird's eye view of the landscape, from Lake Mead and the Colorado River, to the dam to The Strip hotels in the distance, the brave take the plunge and fall to earth at 120mph.
All jumps are tandem jumps and start at $199 including a personal keepsake video of the entire jump. Jumpers can be picked up by a van shuttle at 8am and noon from a central Strip location. The complete session lasts two to three hours and requires that jumpers be in good health, under 240lbs in proportionate weight, and alert.

Flyaway Indoor Skydiving

200 Convention Center Dr. 702-731-4768 or 877-545-8093. www.flyawayindoorskydiving. com. $75, first flight; repeat is $40.

For those who want the thrill of free falling but don't want to do it hurdling to earth from a plane at 2,000 feet, Flyaway Indoor Skydiving might sound like an oxymoron but still provides the 'look ma, no hands' flying experience. First, it's located just off The Strip on Convention Center Drive—no hikes along the freeway to some dirt road in the desert. Second, it's safe: The rewards for bellying up to the ticket box and paying $75 are 20 minutes of instruction, a flight suit and helmet, and a full three minutes suspended in air, no strings attached. An instructor demonstrates how to splay your body for maximum lift, and tuck and roll for maximum crash protection. Then it's off to the padded room where the propeller of a DC3 provides a wind gust of up to 120mph beneath the safety net that separates the flyers on top from a gruesome and grinding demise. Participants *(no more than ten at one time in half-hour segments 10am–10pm daily)* float about 20 feet above the net within a roaring tunnel of pure exhilaration. Do it again the same day for half price. Or, do it with friends and distant relatives; groups get special discounts. Kids under 18 have to be accompanied by a parent and there are height and weight restrictions. Any dangers, however, are more perceived than actual in this contained and controlled environment.

THRILL RIDES

103

WATER FUN

From the pool scene (don't miss the great summer hotel pool events) to beaches with real sand, Las Vegas is getting more wet and wild every day. Here are some great ways to keep cool—or to be cool.

Mandalay Bay Lagoon

At Mandalay Bay,
3950 Las Vegas Blvd. S.
702-632-7777 or 877-632-7000.
www.mandalaybay.com.

Who'd ever thought you could go up a lazy river in Las Vegas? Or spend a day at the beach on The Strip? If you're a guest at Mandalay Bay, you can do both. Named in the press as one of the "sexiest" hotel pools, the 11-acre Mandalay Bay tropical water environment features a sand-and-surf beach

Beach Ball

You don't have to be a hotel guest to enjoy the Mandalay Beach Summer Concert Series that the resort presents each year. For the price of a ticket, you can lie on a towel on the sand, dip your toes in the water, and watch big-name groups (Beach Boys, Chris Isaak, Toto).

Gondolas at Lake Las Vegas

Situated on a private 320-acre lake, Lake Las Vegas Resort has a Mediterranean theme and a small fleet of gondolas plies the lake's placid waters, offering visitors a romantic ride. Outdoor concerts and gourmet food spice up the offering.
220 Grand Mediterra, Henderson.
17mi south of the Las Vegas Strip
via US-95 South. 877-446-6365.
www.gondola.com.

with waves averaging 3–5 feet that can be surfed by body or boogie, a lazy river, three swimming pools, and even a jogging track.

Try floating down the **Lazy River Ride** for three-quarters of a mile on a large inner tube. They don't call it "lazy" for nothing—you'll move at a relaxing snail's pace of about 2mph. Or if you really want to relax, reserve a pricey private bungalow or cabana for the day; they come equipped with snacks, drinks, a television and even a pool attendant to wait on you. Conveniently located on Mandalay Beach, the Temple Bar serves tropical drinks and a healthy selection of food. A fun "beach" casino brings gaming to the sand.

Cool Pools

In Vegas, each resort has a pool personality to match, which makes the town a museum of must-see bodies of water (not to mention the bodies in the water). It started

Mandalay Bay Lagoon

Mandalay Bay Resort & Casino

when Tropicana built a tropical-themed pool, complete with a swim-up blackjack table. Today, Hawaiian faux lava and lush foliage are as common as C-note cabanas with special adult sections that keep the quiet in and kids out.

Hard Rock Hotel – *4455 Paradise Rd., 702-693-4440 or 800-473-7625. www.hardrockhotel.com.* Known for its risqué pool parties, the Hard Rock sends pulsating rock music into the water for a scintillating experience of underwater sound.

Garden of the Gods, Caesars Palace – *3570 Las Vegas Blvd. S. 702-731-7110. www.caesars.com.* Caesars bases its pool area on the Roman baths of Caracalla. Here you'll find three pools in a stunning 4.5-acre area adorned with statues, stones and columns.

Caesars Pool

Caesars Pool

Bellagio Pools – *3600 Las Vegas Blvd. S. 702-693-7111. www.bellagio lasvegas.com.* Bellagio complements its Tuscan-themed resort with six different pools, all surrounded by rose-trellised gardens and fountains. Cabanas here—the priciest in town (expect to pay as much as $300 a day)—are tent-like structures housing a dressing area,

sink, table, six lounge chairs, TV, phone, ceiling fan, mister, and a fridge stocked with fruit platters, water, ice and soft drinks.

Flamingo Las Vegas – *3555 Las Vegas Blvd. S. 702-733-3111. www. flamingolasvegas.com.* Landscaped with waterfalls, slides, ample lounging space, lush gardens and real pink flamingos, the hotel's pool complex shares space with a wildlife habitat where penguins frolic and koi swim.

Four Seasons – *3960 Las Vegas Blvd. S. 702-632-5000. www.foursea sons.com/lasvegas.* The Four Seasons' 8,000-square-foot free-form pool boasts three whirlpools and plenty of decks for lounging. While you sunbathe, attendants spray cooling mist in your face. Four Seasons guests (as well as guests at THEhotel) also have access to the 11-acre sand and surf beach, lazy river ride, exclusive Moorea Beach Club and pools at Mandalay Bay.

MGM Grand – *3799 Las Vegas Blvd. S. 702-891-1111. www.mgmgrand. com.* With 5 pools (including a kiddy pool that's only 1.5feet deep) and a long lazy river for floating inner tubes, the Grand Pool caters to all in its 6.5-acre pool area.

Bare Necessities

A new trend in Vegas's cool pool culture is **Euro-bathing**. You can find these suitless spots at the Moorea Beach Club at Mandalay Bay *(men $30 or more for the privilege)*, Stratosphere, The Palms, Venetian and Caesars Palace. Costs, rules and hours vary.

WATER FUN

FOR KIDS

While much of Las Vegas doesn't kid around—nobody can pretend this is a family setting—there are several attractions and shows in the city that do focus on family fun.

🎡 Adventuredome

*At Circus Circus,
2880 Las Vegas Blvd. S.
702-794-3939 or 877-224-7287.
www.adventuredome.com.
Open year-round Mon–Thu
11am–6pm, Fri–Sat 10am–midnight, Sun 10am–8pm. $4–$7 per
ride. All-day passes, $24.95.*

America's largest indoor theme park, the Adventuredome is a five-acre elevated park located behind the west tower of Circus Circus. It features the world's only indoor double-loop, double-corkscrew roller coaster—the **Canyon Blaster**—which reaches a top speed of 55mph. Set in a Grand Canyon motif, the Adventuredome goes out of its way to ensure that visitors get their "piece of the rock" when it comes to entertainment, packing 19 attractions under its glass dome. Since opening its doors in 1993 with four rides, the Adventuredome has welcomed more than 15 million visitors. Besides the Canyon Blaster, other top attractions include the **Rim Runner** boat ride, which climaxes in a 60-foot water plunge, and **Fun House Express**, in which Chaos whirls riders in all three dimensions of motion, and the Inverter turns riders upside down. Team-laser-tag enthusiasts will want to head for **Lazer Blast**. Adventurers of all ages flock to the **Extreme Zone** to climb walls, bounce into the air on a "bungee trampoline" or try their skill at Pike's Pass, with 18 holes of miniature golf.

> ### Adventuredome Facts
> - The dome is 200 feet high.
> - Adventuredome is enclosed by 8,615 panes of glass, each weighing over 300 pounds.
> - Adventuredome took a year to build and cost $90 million.

Adventuredome Theme Park

Adventuredome Theme Park

MUST DO

ibles that go as high as $2,500 (for one-of-a-kind items such as memorabilia from Coca-Cola-sponsored NASCAR events).

🎮 Gameworks

At Showcase Mall,
3769 Las Vegas Blvd. S.
702-432-4263.
www.gameworks.com.
Open year-round Sun–Thu 10am–midnight, Fri–Sat 10am–1am.

A unique high-tech entertainment destination where you can eat, drink, party and experience state-of-the-art interactive attractions, Gameworks knows how to push the fun button for each member of the family. Here you'll find more than 200 of the newest games, many designed exclusively for Gameworks, as well as old-fashioned pinball machines. These include multisensory games based on the movies *Star Wars* and *Jurassic Park*, as well as Indy 500, Ford Racing Zone, and VR2002 Roller Coaster. There's even a five-story climbing wall. Gameworks also features a high-energy bar area (a good place for parents to take a break) and a full-service restaurant.

Brian Jones

Adventuredome

If you'd like a high-tech motion-simulator ride, then the **IMAX Ridefilm Cineplex** is nearby, featuring IMAX ReBoot: The Ride and other films that take you on a warp-speed journey through cyberspace, using the Ridefilm system's computer-generated images.

Everything Coca-Cola Retail Store Las Vegas

At Showcase Mall,
3785 Las Vegas Blvd. S.
800-810-2653.
Open year-round daily 10am–11pm.

If you want to keep the kids content, show them the bottle—the 100-foot-tall trademark Coca-Cola bottle in front of Monte Carlo's on The Strip. On two floors here you'll find everything you can imagine that has to do with Coke. A soda fountain on the second floor offers ice-cream floats and other concoctions made with Coke. Here you can buy everything from a $1 souvenir to collect-

Babes in Adventureland

The Adventuredome has many attractions suitable for younger children, including the traditional carousel, a roller coaster (Miner Mike) and Cliffhangers, a play-space with crawl-through tunnels, slides and more. The park offers bumper cars, carnival-style games, clown shows, arcade games and a snack bar.

FOR KIDS

107

M&M's World Las Vegas

*At Showcase Mall,
3785 Las Vegas Blvd. S.
702-736-7611. www.mymms.com.
Open year-round Sun–Thu 9am–
11pm, Fri–Sat 9am–midnight.*

Sweet smells and tastes await
you at M&M's World—a four-story
monument to chocolate. Each
floor of this interactive shopping
and retail complex offers a different layer of M&M's brand merchandise items—truly a chocolate-
lover's dream.

You won't want to miss the M&M's
Racing Team Shop; Colorworks,
where you can sample 21 different colors of plain and peanut
M&Ms; and Ethel M Chocolates,
the ultimate gourmet chocolate
boutique. And be sure to check
out the fourth-floor ice-cream/
candy shop. *I Lost My M In Vegas*,
a complimentary 3D interactive
movie, plays seven days a week on
the third floor. Kids who "enroll" at
M&M Academy may even take part
in the movie.

Tournament of Kings
Excalibur Hotel & Casino

Tournament of Kings

*At Excalibur. 3850 Las Vegas Blvd. S.
702-597-7600 or 800-937-7777.
www.excaliburcasino.com.
Shows nightly 6pm & 8:30pm.
$58.24, dinner included.*

When was the last time you
attended a kids' dinner theater?
At the Tournment of Kings at
Excalibur, it's the order of the day.
A finger-licking good meal goes
hand-in-hand with a genuine
jousting tournament and great
special effects, including dragons
and fire wizards. It all makes this
show a royal treat for the entire
family.

The story begins when King Arthur
gathers his fellow kings of Europe
for a no-holds-barred competition to honor his son. Rival kings
begin the games, gallantly riding
their faithful steeds through round
upon round of the medieval sport,
testing their agility, strength and
endurance.

Beware: As the event winds down
and the victorious king takes his

M&M's World Las Vegas
Brian Jones

celebration lap, an evil wizard, Mordred, attacks, dampening the festivities and threatening to throw the world of Avalon into an age of fire and shadow.

Kingdoms clash, beasts attack and the fire of combat burns bright. Arthur is mortally wounded, but before he dies, he asks his son (the show takes some artistic license with the original tale) to avenge his death.

Medieval Village

If you trade in your horse for a ride on a tall escalator, you'll find yourself on Excalibur's second floor, walking straight into a fairytale medieval village.

Wonderful shops (some offering medieval-style merchandise), restaurants (including a delicious buffet), and costumed strolling singers, musicians and jugglers add to the lively atmosphere. In the midst of it all, a stage area offers free shows, including puppetry, music, storytelling and juggling. On the hotel's lower level is the Fantasy Faire midway, a carnival labyrinth of games, as well as the SpongeBob 4D EFX Ride.

★The Lion Habitat

At MGM Grand,
3799 Las Vegas Blvd. S.
877-880-0880.
www.mgmgrand.com.
Open year-round daily 11am–
10pm. Free.

Las Vegas may not have a zoo, but it certainly has its share of lions. The three-story Lion Habitat at MGM Grand houses a variety of African lions and cubs, including Goldie, Metro and Baby Lion. You'll see the big cats from all angles in the glass-enclosed 5,345-square-foot structure, as you walk through the see-through tunnel that runs through the habitat. And it's all free of charge.

MGM Grand/Mirage

The Lion Habitat

★The Secret Garden of Siegfried & Roy

At The Mirage, 3400 Las Vegas Blvd.
702-791-7111 or 800-627-6667.
www.themirage.com.
Open year-round daily Mon–Fri
11am–5:30pm, weekends
10am–5:30pm. $15 adults,
$10 children (ages 4-12).

You'll think you're in the jungle when you enter this lush 15-acre refuge, complete with palm trees, flowers, waterfalls and the calls of exotic birds and jungle drums

FOR KIDS

The Secret Garden of Siegfried & Roy

Brian Jones

playing in the background. Here you'll find Royal white tigers, white lions, Bengal tigers, snow leopards and more.

Adjoining the garden is the **Dolphin Habitat**, featuring four connecting pools with a sand bottom and an artificial reef. These simulate the natural environment for a group of dolphins that reside here. You can tour the habitat, which provides a sanctuary for Atlantic bottlenose dolphins and also serves as a breeding facility, to watch trainers interact with the gentle mammals.

To truly indulge those flipper fantasies, kids can tap into Mirage's **Dolphin Trainer for a Day** program. It's a hands-on experience of learning about this fascinating creature through the Dolphin Habitat. Participants don wet suits and jump in the water with the trainers and dolphins for some photos and bottle-nosed kisses after they have learned all the hand-signals and spent time getting to know their designated dolphin. The experience takes about six hours and comes with a gourmet lunch. Group sizes are limited. The program costs $500

per person. *Reservations must be made well in advance or through the Mirage concierge desk.*

Feeding Frenzy at Atlantis Aquarium

At The Forum Shops at Caesars Palace, 3570 Las Vegas Blvd. S. 702-893-3807. www.robertwynn.com/FishAq.htm. Tours daily at 1:15pm & 5:15pm.

More than 500 individual fish representing some 100 different species call this 50,000-gallon aquarium home. Make sure you drop by at 3:15pm or 7:15pm, when you can watch divers enter the tank and feed the sharks, rays and other denizens of the deep. The aquarium also offers a below-the-scenes tour of the support facilities during the week. *Dive shows and tours are free of charge.*

Fish Stories at Silverton

3333 Blue Diamond Rd. 702-263-7777 or 866-946-4373. www.silvertoncasino.com.

Silverton's 117,000-gallon inner reef is home to more than 4,000 exotic fish, including stingrays

MUST DO

and sharks. A marine biologist feeds them thrice daily *(1:30pm, 4:30pm and 7:30pm)* as he talks to the audience from inside the tank. Check out the Mermaid Lounge for a mesmerizing moment with jellyfish.

Pole Position Raceway

4175 South Arville, 702-227-7223. www.polepositionraceway.com. Adult races: $25 per race; Children: $22.

Put Junior's go-kart fantasies on steroids at Pole Position. This quarter-mile, Euro-inspired indoor track just west of The Strip features electric EK20, 18-horsepower go-karts that kick. The track winds through the 60,000 square foot facility supporting some 58 go-karts in all, racing each other for time relays and reporting results in blazing lights on the wall. Each racer's speed is tracked as they careen and bump at top speeds of 45mph. No wreckages here, just a rollicking good time.

Wild Rides at Primm

Primm Valley Resorts, 31900 Las Vegas Blvd. S., Primm 702-386-7867 or 1-800-FUN-STOP. www.primmvalleyresorts.com. Open Mon–Fri, noon–8pm, Fri–Sat 10am–midnight, Sun 10am–10pm. All day unlimited rides: $30; half-day $22.

This resort at the California border with Nevada is actually three casino hotels: Buffalo Bill's, Primm Valley, and Whiskey Pete's. They are all connected by a monorail running between the properties. Hailing from the days when Vegas promoters pictured the city as

a family kind of town, Primm Valley Resorts grabbed the flag and put kids on coasters, drops, and all sorts of rides that only a child can love. Starting with the **Desperado**, Primm has amusement and thrill attractions, three hotel casinos, as well as shopping, golf and entertainment just 40 minutes south of the city. The Desperado is still one of the top thrill rides around town and ranks among the top ten in the country for height and speed. It climbs to an altitude of 209 feet, tops speeds of 80mph, delivers more than 5 Gs and lasts a heart-pounding 2.43 minutes with nine moments of total weightlessness. A ride costs $8 and riders must be at least 48 inches tall.

Then there's the **Turbo Drop** that flies into the face of gravity rather than away from it. It's a plunge straight down, from 170 feet in the air, at an intense 45mph and costs $6. It lasts about a minute—45 seconds to climb and 15 seconds, which feel like an hour, to shoot back down.

The Adventure Canyon Log Flume continues the action with swirling rapids and treacherous waterfalls inside a Wild West scenario. Riders shoot laser guns at targets and bad guys as they fly by for a moment of marksmanship as well as exhilaration. The ride lasts four minutes and costs $6.

The Vault is there for those who want to take their dares from the safety of their chairs. Viewers can choose from thrill different experiences and move through them in a 3-D High Def Digital projection motion simulator ride that is the state of the art for the technology these days *(admission $6)*.

FOR KIDS

111

SHOPPING

Like everything else in Las Vegas, the city has taken a favored pastime and turned it gold. Shopping is not about finding a blouse or that perfect pair of shoes. It is about passing into a sort of twilight browsers' zone where store merchandise is just a sideline to the real entertainment to be found amid opera trios performing in St. Mark's Square, flirtations with buff Roman sentries on the Appian Way, mehendi tattoos offered in Moorish courtyards, or coffee overlooking a catwalk of swaggering fashion models. Shops in Las Vegas see 50,000 people stroll by each day to catch the mall-made action along fantastical promenades ranging from 500,000 to nearly two million square feet. So it is no surprise that shopping has taken its place high on the list of top reasons people visit Las Vegas—just under "pleasure."

▲ The Forum Shops at Caesars Palace

At Caesars Palace,
3570 Las Vegas Blvd. S.
702-893-4800. www.caesars.
com/Caesars/LasVegas.

It's said that all roads lead to Rome. If the foot traffic in The Forum Shops is any indication, that adage rings true. With more than 160 stores, the 675,000-square-foot mall attracts as many as 200,000 visitors on a busy day. No wonder it's billed as the most successful shopping center in the country in terms of sales volume per square foot.

The merchandise mix offers everything from high fashion to novelty items. From Longchamp to Fendi and from Anthropologie to Escada, the Forum Shops is one of the wonders of Las Vegas. The

The Forum Shops

Brian Jones, Las Vegas News Bureau/LVCVA

Amen Wardy Home Store features an unusual selection of items for the home. Estee Lauder allows customers to experiment on their own with a full line of make-up.

More Roads to Rome

Forum Shops grew another mini-city in 2004. The ornate, three-tiered extension added to the collection of upscale specialty stores and restaurants with Varvatos, Bruno Magli and Longchamps. The unusual centerpiece here is the circular elevator, but that takes a back seat to the facades of ancient Rome that line the lengthy promenades and the animated statuary and special effects that come to life each hour around two otherwise sleepy Forum fountains.

MUST DO

Of course, FAO Schwartz is a blast for kids of all ages.

The mall contains 13 restaurants and specialty food shops, including two Wolfgang Puck restaurants: **Spago**, his signature property, and **Chinois**, his Asian-fusion delight. Also find Joe's Seafood, BOA, Sushi Roku, Prime Steakhouse and even Pinkberry. As the meals melt from lunch to dinner the sky turns from dawn to dusk in an ever changing Roman firmament that never sees the true light of day.

★Miracle Mile

Surrounding (and connected to)
Planet Hollywood,
3663 Las Vegas Blvd. S.
702-866-0710 or 888-800-8284.
www.miraclemileshopslv.com.

What could be more fitting than a Miracle Mile of shopping encircling Planet Hollywood. For joggers and power walkers, the mall is, indeed, an entertaining mile of merchandise—many purposely ensconced in this location because of their Los Angeles links or affiliations. Stores such as Sur La Table, Swarovski, Tommy

Mai Oh Mai

Trader Vic's tore down its legendary Beverly Hills tiki hut location in April 2007 and opened up at the Miracle Mile in June. The 1955 grass hut landmark may be gone from LA but the Mai Tai lives on. The sweet, refreshing rum cocktail was created by Victor Jules "Trader Vic" Bergeron in 1944 and introduced to the Hawaiian islands in the 1950s. Tahitian for "the very best," Mai Tai became the slogan for his entire operation, which eventually grew to number 29 Polynesian-themed restaurants around the world.

Bahama, BCBG, Bettie Page have found a fun home in Las Vegas next to the hippest new hotel on The Strip. Some interesting kiosks and stores remain from the mall's original incarnation as the Desert Passage, which made it a Disneyesque experience of ancient Arabia amid faux medinas and interior desert landscape designs. You can still find rug merchants and mahendi artists and fine art boutiques among the chains. Restaurants provide all manner of

Miracle Mile Shops, Planet Hollywood

choices from sushi buffets to oyster bars to cheeseburger heaven. Browsers can also stop for a full body massage by hydrojets ($10 for 15 minutes), backrubs by shiatsu chairs ($1 for three minutes) and real time advice (free!) by the wise manager who moonlights as a physiotherapist and kung fu teacher at Zen Zone.

Grand Canal Shoppes

At The Venetian,
3355 Las Vegas Blvd. S.
702-414-1000 or 877-883-6423.
www.venetian.com.

Pigeons are all that's needed to make this Venice shopping experience feel any more real (the birds are there, but luckily they're outside the hotel).
Strolling down the cobblestone walkways of this 500,000-square-foot indoor mall at the Venetian, along nearly a quarter-mile of Venice's famed Grand Canal, you'll encounter more than 70 stores and boutiques. Many of the Grand

Street performer, Grand Canal Shoppes

The Venetian

Over the Top

Looking for luxury in Las Vegas? The Shoppes at Palazzo take high end spending to a new level with 450,000 square feet of uber-designer shopping anchored by the city's first Barneys New York. Manolo Blahnik, Jimmy Choo, Stella McCartney, True Religion—60 international shops. It all connects to the Canal Shoppes for a million square feet of upscale shopping in one hot spot.

Canal Shoppes have premiered here for the first time in the US market.
At St. Mark's Square (where the pigeons are found in the real Venice), you can take a 15-minute gondola ride down the 1,200-foot-long **Grand Canal★** and be serenaded by a singing gondolier.
Even if you skip the gondola ride, know that the shopping is a trip in itself. Be sure to visit Il Prato, which carries collectible masks and fine paper goods (including colorful glass-point fountain pens), and Ripa de Monti, which offers Venetian glass and collectibles. Another must-see store is Sephora, a 10,000-square-foot beauty emporium dedicated to women's perfumes and cosmetics.
Lladro, Tolstoys and Ancient Creations are also fun to browse for gifts. Wonderful cafés and restaurants, many of them with canalside seating, are located in this retail area.
As in Europe you can have your pick of gelatos here. Fashion concierges provide personalized shopping advice, by appointment only, to international guests who do not speak English.

⚜ Fashion Show Mall

3200 Las Vegas Blvd. S., at the intersection of Las Vegas Blvd. & Spring Mountain Rd., across from Wynn Las Vegas. 702-369-8382. www.thefashionshow.com.

Whoever said that "bigger is better" must have seen the new Fashion Show Mall.

The first mall to open on The Strip, the venue holds the distinction of being not only its largest shopping establishment but, thanks to a recent expansion, one of the largest shopping centers in the nation. In 2006, the premier retail venue completed a four-year, $1 billion redevelopment, which more than doubled its size to approximately two million square feet.

The renovation included expanded flagship department stores from Neiman-Marcus and Macy's, along with new stores from Saks Fifth Avenue, a prototype Bloomingdale's Home and Nevada's first Nordstrom. It is expected that ultimately the mall will be anchored by eight major department stores. Find the Apple Store here, and the only tapas restaurant in town

with a view of The Strip. On warm days, the 480-foot "cloud" structure above a 72,000-square-foot plaza on The Strip come in handy for its shade producing effects.

At night it presents multimedia fashion images and projections of live fashion shows. Snackers can dine at the 1,500-seat food court or try the California Pizza Kitchen, the Café at Nordstrom or Mariposa at Neiman Marcus hidden away between the more than 200 boutiques and stores.

The mall hosts regular fashion shows on its catwalk area, often sponsored by tenant stores and featuring a charity angle.

> **Sundries in the Mall**
> Omni Chemists is a great place to stop if you're looking for sundry items that run the gamut from the unusual to the unheard-of. If you've been looking for Monkey Brand Tooth Powder from India, look no more. You've found it… along with countless cosmetics, vitamins and other obscure and unique imported items, including great suntan products.

Ladieswear catwalk, Fashion Show Mall

SHOPPING

Le Boulevard

At Paris Las Vegas,
3655 Las Vegas Blvd. S.
702-946-7000 or 800-634-3434.
www.parislv.com.

Le Boulevard cries out from every storefront, Vive la différence! The distinct French flavor is immediately apparent when you enter this 31,000-square-foot retail space that connects Paris to its sister resort, Bally's, beginning at one casino and ending at the other. This French connection is called Le Boulevard and consists of authentic French boutiques in a chic simulated Parisian setting.

Walk through the archway to Paris, where you will be greeted by the sight of cobblestone streets, winding alleyways and Parisian street lamps. One of the highlights is **Napoleon's**, a club featuring live entertainment, a cigar lounge and a walk-in humidor.

Some of the shops you won't want to miss include Les Mémoires, a bed and bath shop offering everything from soaps to candles; and Les Eléments, a garden shop with fresh and dried flowers, topiaries, statues, pottery and French linens. La Cave offers private label and premium French wines and gourmet foods and cheeses.

Lenôtre, named for culinary master Gaston **Lenôtre**, features fresh-baked croissants, breads and pastries, as well as chocolates and fruit preserves. Then there's Le Journal, a 24-hour hotel gift shop, and Presse, a reproduction of a French magazine kiosk selling newspapers and magazines.

A children's store, Les Enfants, offers French toys and games and also carries a line of children's apparel.

Be sure to check out Judith Jack, a boutique that boasts one of the most extensive collections of designer Jack's sterling silver and marcasite jewelry, handbags and watches.

Street performers, Le Boulevard

Paris Las Vegas

 Mandalay Place

*At Mandalay Bay,
3950 Las Vegas Blvd. S.
702-632-9325 or 800-632-7000.
www.mandalayplace.com.*

Home to 41 unusual and quirky shops and a seasoning of top-shelf restaurants, the newest mall in Las Vegas is located on a skybridge between Mandalay Bay and Luxor. Here you'll find The Strip's only book shop, **The Reading Room**, with a hearty set of Las Vegas guides to match its strength in best sellers and magazines. The adjacent coffee bar, with tables surrounding the bookstore's entrance, creates the perfect spot for some rest and relaxation when you need a break from gaming. Find flirty confections in Nora Blue,

clever toys in Five Little Monkeys, wowing and eco-sensitive furnishings at Lik Design, gems for Fido at LUSHPUPPY, and casual designer duds at Just Cavalli.

Via Bellagio

*At Bellagio, 3600 Las Vegas Blvd. S.
702-693-7111.
www.bellagioresort.com.*

It's no secret that Prada, Chanel and the fashion designs of Lagerfeld, Georgio Armani and Hermès always go into freestanding stores. Now, for the first time, thanks to Bellagio, you can find them all under one roof.

Via Bellagio's inviting collection of upscale boutiques and shops combines the timeless with the avant-garde, the simple with the extravagant. Full collections from the designers mentioned above, as well as from Gucci, Yves St. Laurent, and Tiffany & Co., are here for the taking. Besides high fashion, you'll also find elegant jewelry, watches and gifts.

Bellagio

Via Bellagio

NIGHTLIFE

If Las Vegas has anything, it has nightlife. Call it all-night life. Clubs in this town do not get going until at least 11pm and when they do the action often lasts until 4am. Don't be surprised if you encounter a velvet rope or two on your club jaunts.

This is the land of the "ultra lounge" where model wannabes in slinky dark dresses serve $1,000 bottles of champagne, where you have to plunk down a Platinum Card before you find a seat and to get anywhere near that seat you might have to let go of a C-note or two. But Vegas will show you a good time in return with special effects creating dizzying images on the dance floor, wowing pool scenes, plenty of celebrity appeal and a cocktail culture that proffers $3,000 drinks accessorized by diamond-studded straws. If it is scene you want, it is scene you will get. And this scene is like no other.

Body English

At the Hard Rock Hotel, 4455 Paradise Rd. 702-693-4000, www.bodyenglish.com. Open weekends, 10:30pm–4am.

If you want to party like a rock star, you can under the baccarat crystal chandeliers, between the mirrored walls and around the rich leather furnishings of this bachelor pad come nightclub. The Hilton sisters, Carmen Electra, Kanye West, Christina Aguilera… these are just a few of the sightings. But celebrity has its downside—stiff covers, long waits (two hours is average) if

you don't appeal to the bouncer's tastes, and drinking with the plebs if you are not on the VIP list. Enjoy faux fog atmosphere on the dance floor, $2,000 martinis and crowds galore. Squint hard, everyone looks like a celeb here.

⚓ Ghost Bar

At the Palms Casino Resort, 4321 W. Flamingo Rd. 702-942-7777 or 866-725-6773. www.palms.com. Open daily 8pm until late.

Billing itself as "the ultimate apparition," the Ghost Bar at the Palms is

Ghost Bar

Palms Casino Resort

a sultry and sophisticated indoor-outdoor lounge and skydeck on the 55th floor of the hotel with a spectacular 360-degree view of Las Vegas.

You may have a close encounter of the celebrity kind here: The long list of notables that have visited the Ghost Bar includes Heather Locklear, Carmen Electra, Don Johnson and Nicolas Cage. If celebrity sightings aren't exciting enough for you, try the glass inset in the floor of the skydeck, which offers a jaw-dropping, straight-down view. The 8,000-square-foot venue has a 30-foot ghost-shaped soffit in the ceiling, which changes colors as a DJ spins a mix of music. Floor-to-ceiling windows and custom, ultra-contemporary lounge furniture decorate the room. Seek privacy in the intimate seating arrangements or mingle at the terrazzo bar.

Stoney's Rockin' Country

9155 Las Vegas Blvd. S. 702-435-BULL (4855). www.stoneysrockincountry.com.

Vegas being Vegas, even country bars and Texas two-step joints have morphed into a new kind of back-at-the-ranch experience: the Cowboy Ultra-Lounge. Stoney's Rockin' Country, runs Tuesdays through Saturdays with doors opening at 7pm. The colossal 20,000-square-foot nightclub can fit 1,000 people and has a dance floor the size of a barn, plus the requisite mechanical bull, coin-op pool tables, two full-service bars, a cowboy arcade, a three-lane bowling alley, a $250,000 sound system, go-go

I'll Have One of Those
The Ghost Bar's signature **Ghostini** cocktail blends Absolut vodka, Midori and sour mix.

girls and a VIP ultra-lounge for cowboys with discerning tastes. It also has ladies nights, $20 all-you-can-drink draught specials and live acts such as the Thunder Road Band and Toby Keith's opening act, Flynville Train.

JET Nightclub

At The Mirage, 3400 Las Vegas Blvd. S. 702-791-7111 or 800-627-6667. www.jetlv.com. Open Fri, Sat & Mon. 10:30pm–4:30am.

Jet features a one-of-a-kind light and laser grid, state-of-the-art cryogenic-effects systems, and what the owners tout as the best sound-design technology available. Three distinct rooms each has its own dance floor, DJ booth and sound system. The

Word on Wine
Las Vegas is fast becoming known for its magnificent wine collections. The **Wine Cellar** at **Rio** has a 50,000-bottle collection that includes such rare vintages as a c. 1800 Madeira from Thomas Jefferson's cellar, a prize bottle of 1924 Château Mouton Rothschild, and the world's largest selection of Chateau d'Yquem, valued at $2 million. You can taste more than 100 wines by the glass here or simply watch the glass—**Aureole** at Mandalay Bay has a four-story, glass wine tower where tethered "wine angels," scale and pull from the 10,000-bottle collection.

main room presents a mix of rock, hip-hop, and popular dance music. A second room is dedicated to house music spun by international DJs, while in the third room you can hear an eclectic mix of music spanning the decades from the early years of rock through the 1980s. Four full-service bars offer specialty cocktails, and the Light group's signature (and pricey) European bottle service is featured in each room of the club.

🍸 Pure

At Caesars Palace,
3570 S. Las Vegas Blvd. S.
702-731-7873 or 800-634-6661.
www.caesars.com.
Open Fri–Sun & Tue 10pm–4am.

Owned by Andre Agassi, Steffi Graf, Shaquille O'Neal and Celine Dion, the 36,000-square-foot nightclub consists of three distinct environments. The main room is draped in shades of snow, cream, egg shell and silver. Three bars here do the mixing beneath a raised VIP area and next to a dance floor surrounded by oversized cushions. Dressed in steamy shades of crimson, the Red Room is reserved for the moneyed crowd, secluded from the main club with its own bar and VIP restrooms. Lush draperies, chandeliers and upholstered walls, and cozy private pods complete the sense of being sequestered.

A glass elevator leads up to the Terrace, a 14,000-square-foot hideaway presenting panoramic views of The Strip amid cabanas, tables and a crowded dance floor.

A recent addition, the famous Pussycat Dolls Lounge adjoins the larger nightclub, bringing the group's well-noted art of seduction and circumstance to the club. Guests are teased throughout the night by Dolls dropping from the ceiling on swings, swaggering around chairs and props and singing and dancing onstage.

Rain Nightclub

At the Palms Casino Resort,
4321 W. Flamingo Rd.
702-942-7777 or 866-725-6773.
www.palms.com.
Open Thu 11pm–5am, Fri–Sat 10pm–5am.

If you want to see rain in the desert, you're going to have to go to the Palms. In fact, for a real rainwater experience, try one of the venue's eight water booths, which feature patent-leather banquettes filled with water.

Rain is the ultimate contemporary nightclub and concert venue. It combines performances by international headliners with an electrifying dance club, a private-event facility and intimate enclaves in one dynamic multisensory experience. From the moment you enter through the gold-mirrored mosaic tunnel, which is filled with changing light, fog and sound, you know you're in for a downpour of special effects. Inside, a water

Rain NightClub

Palms Casino Resort

wall, a rain curtain, fog, haze and pyrotechnics such as 16-foot fire plumes add to the atmosphere. Luxury, private and VIP accommodations include a cabana level with private cabanas seating eight to 12 guests. Each cabana includes a liquid-crystal display screen, lights that change colors, a mini-bar and specialty furniture. High above the cabanas, six lavish skyboxes boast private balconies overlooking the nightclub below.

Risqué

At Paris Las Vegas,
3655 Las Vegas Blvd. S.
702-946-4589. www.risquelv.com.
Open Thu–Sun 10pm until late.

This ultra-lounge features a dessert bar with one-of-a-kind creations, prepared by renowned pastry chef Jean-Claude Canestrier. Here tropical fruit tempura and orange blossom crème brûlée share the menu with soufflés and flambés, distinctive coffee drinks, premium cocktails, a wide selection of sakes, and a carefully chosen wine list. From the sweet confections to the plush overstuffed couches on balconies overlooking the Las Vegas Strip, this club seeks to create the ultimate "night culture." Geared towards a sophisticated crowd, this ultra-lounge seeks out the chic in terms of its music, service and décor.

Risqué has a raised, lighted dance floor, a stylish Salon Privée with a cocktail bar, a dessert bar (alongside the intimate dance floor), and a select late-night menu in Ah Sin downstairs.

French velvet drapes, crystal chandeliers and mirrored lighting effects enhance the atmosphere at Risqué. Even the restrooms at Risqué are remarkable—a translucent wall separates the men's and women's restrooms, each of which features iridescent tile.

Lucky Strike Lanes

At The Rio, 3700 W. Flamingo Rd.
702-777-7999. www.riolasvegas.
com. Open Mon–Fri 2pm–3am,
Sat, Sun 11am–3am. Patrons must
be over 21 after 9pm.

Lucky Strike puts a new spin on grandpa's game. Don't expect to rent a lane for $25 and throw in the bowling shoes for $5. The velvet rope comes out at night, the dress code is definitely R to X and the games are hot hot hot. You can toast your ten-pin strike with Dom Perignon and those hard plastic

Bring it Downtown

For an unusual experience of the night in Vegas try Downtown. **Fremont Street East**, just beyond the "Vivavision" corridor of the Fremont Street Experience, brings a new pedestrian promenade of clubs and action, starting with the Beauty Bar, where you can sip martinis and get a manicure in a throbbing club of music and mayhem. The Griffin has a medieval angle that will appeal to goths and hipsters. Coyote Ugly opened Hogs and Heifers, where rowdiness is a good thing. The Atomic Liquors cocktail Lounge and the Downtown Cocktail Room offer a more mellow melange. It all happens around a swirl of flashing signage and lights that is the Neon Museum, a living museum of Vegas neon signage of old, given new life along this cocktail corridor and blinking all night long.

chairs are soft, plush leather here. Chances are you'll be playing with strangers by the end of the night, no matter who's keeping score.

Studio 54

At the MGM Grand,
3799 Las Vegas Blvd. S.
702-891-7279 or 800-929-1111.
www.studio54lv.com.
Open Tue–Sat 10pm until late.

A high-energy trend-setting nightclub, Studio 54, named for the late, great New York City venue, claims to feature the most eclectic music mix in the country, combined with state-of-the-art sound, lighting and staging. Music, courtesy of a DJ, ranges from cutting-edge sounds to the songs of the 1970s that made the original Studio 54 the epicenter of pop culture and style. The 22,000-square-foot nightclub offers four dance floors and bars, an exclusive area on the second floor for invited guests, as well as several semi-private lounges. If you're lucky, you might see one of the surprise acts (in the past these have included the Go-

Confetti on the dancefloor at Studio 54

MGM Mirage/Grand

Gos and Prince) that take the stage on any given evening.

Tabu

At the MGM Grand,
3799 Las Vegas Blvd. S.
702-891-7816 or 800-929-1111.
www.mgmgrand.com.
Open Tue–Sun 10pm–dawn.

Symbolizing everything chic, cosmopolitan and innovative, Tabu's design is a distinct combination of modern fashion and refined style. A comfortable level of vocals allows guests to carry on conversations while taking in the scene and enjoying a cocktail. Although there's no dance floor, guests have been known to boogie on the 700-pound concrete tables—which, as luck would have it, house projected imagery systems that react to motion.
That makes for quite an interactive scene. Just laying a glass down on the table causes the under-lying image on the table to change. Three distinct rooms here cater to every mood. The main room with its reactive tables has a large bar and a DJ booth. In the back of the club, the discreet Champagne Bar is decorated with a cool animated mural of the desert.
You can reserve the circular Tantra Room, with its own bar and black marble floor, for private parties.

Christian Audigier

At TI, 3300 Las Vegas Blvd. S.
702-466-9723 or 800-944-7444.
www.audigierlv.com.
Open Thu–Sun 10pm until dawn.

Part tattoo parlor, part South Beach sheen, the new Christian Audigier night scene at TI does

Tao

not cast even a sliver of orange in the shadows of the space formerly known as Tangerine.

That's because Audigier, the heretofore French clothing designer of Melrose Avenue in Hollywood, puts the Ed Hardy, "skull and roses" tattoo art of his clothing brands all over the new Strip scene spot. It's a Goth world inside—silver skulls looming over the shiny black faux croc leather banquettes, backed by heavy vermillion velvet drapery that one might find in a haunted house or, say, a cathouse, all dramatically offset by two illuminated 1,000-gallon tanks full of jellyfish

Outside, the patio setting over the Pirate's Cove is all white with plush cushions, clean lines, patio attire you might find in finer homes. But the seats are some of the hottest on The Strip.

Audigier's label-mania extends to libations with his own lines of wines from vineyards in the South of France. As with most ultra-lounges in Las Vegas, you won't sit unless you pay the price, usually a C-note or three .... for a bottle.

Tao

At The Venetian, 3355 Las Vegas Blvd. S. 702-388-8338 or 877-283-6423. www.venetian.com. Open Thu–Sat 10:30pm–5:30am.

Los Angeles glitterati favor this 40,000-square-foot "Asian City," a multifaceted and multistory venue housing a restaurant, an ultra-lounge and a nightclub. Among the highlights of the $20 million, Zen-like dining and entertainment complex are an outside terrace with Strip views. It has two rooms: The Temple and The Emperors Ballroom, each with its own varied music format; eight private sky boxes with mini-bars, espresso machines, and banquettes outfitted with secure purse drawers. Then there's the European bottle service, and state-of-the-art everything—from lighting to sound to multimedia projection. A chic ultra-lounge serves as a gathering spot for cocktails and conversation, while the 10,000-square-foot Tao Nightclub pulses with energy. Summers get a boost from the heat with pool cabana service at night for those who want to shell out a grand for sitting and service.

NIGHTLIFE

SPAS

It's touch and glow at Las Vegas resorts these days when it comes to the extravagant spas that almost every major property houses. From massage to relaxation techniques, you'll definitely get the royal treatment.

🌿 Aqua Sulis

At JW Marriott Las Vegas Resort & Spa, 221 N. Rampart Blvd. 702-869-7777 or 877-869-8777. www.marriott.com.

Set in a scenic desert sanctuary 20 minutes away from The Strip (next to Red Rock National Preserve), Aqua Sulis fosters an indoor/outdoor experience focusing on the healing powers of water. Prepare for your treatment by hitting the soak and plunge pools—especially refreshing in the hot summer months—that line a landscaped patio area outside the 40,000-square-foot spa. The battery of hot soaks, cold soaks, jets that nail nearly every muscle in your body, and a menu of treatments that run from European to exotic make coming here well worth the trip. Energized spa-goers can hit the gym, where two-story floor-to-ceiling windows overlook the pool and desert, or take advantage of Tai Chi, Pilates and yoga classes.

🌿 Canyon Ranch Spa-Club at The Venetian

3355 Las Vegas Blvd. S. 702-414-3600 or 877-220-2688. www.canyonranch.com.

Meanwhile, back at the ranch, Canyon Ranch at the Venetian to be precise, the well-known name in health resorts is welcoming people to their first SpaClub in Las Vegas. This peaceful and plush

Canyon Ranch Spa Club

The Venetian

facility offers more than 120 spa services. It also features a fitness facility with a wellness center staffed by physicians and nutritionists. Canyon Ranch Salon *(4th floor)* offers a full list of beauty services from haircuts to full makeovers. With the opening of Palazzo adjacent to the Venetian, the Canyon Ranch facility connects the two properties with an added 65,000 square feet of pure pleasure space to become the largest hotel spa in Las Vegas, if not the US.

Spa & Salon Bellagio

3600 La Vegas Blvd. S. 702-694-7444 or 888-987-6667. www.bellagio.com.

Spa & Salon Bellagio has been a long time coming. The resort that changed the face of Las Vegas when it opened in 1998 has done it again—this time with a new 65,000-square-foot spa that counts 56 treatment rooms and 12 skin-care rooms, making it the largest pampering palace in town to date.

Located in the recent 33-story tower addition, the spa sports an elegant design with clean lines, the colors of natural stone and private candlelit places to meditate. You'll find reflecting pools and waterwalls throughout, and an infusion of cool jades and hand-blown glass in the calming spaces. A private Watsu pool room allows for the special namesake stretching treatment that simulates being back in the womb. For the ultimate in opulence, the Egyptian Gold treatment leaves the body exfoliated, moisturized and glowing with a dusting of real gold.

Qua Spa at Caesars Palace

3570 Las Vegas Blvd. S.
702-731-7110 or 800-634-6661.
www.harrahs.com/casinos/
caesars-palace.

The sybaritic pleasures to be found here along the second floor of the new Augustus Tower take time to assimilate. And time is what you need here, to soak in the mineral-infused waters of the indoor cleansing pools: the Tepidarium, Caldarium and Frigidarium calibrated at 98, 104 and 72 degrees. Water jets and deluge showers hit the muscles and calm the nerves. Treatments range from herb garden oil massages to Swarovrski crystal treatments that keep the body in sparkle for five days. Complement your massage with a sweaty sit in the sauna followed by a frozen few moments in the spa's arctic chamber, where snow blows in the purple-silver glow. Top it off with a choice of tea, attended to by the spa's tea concierge.

The Spa at Green Valley Ranch

2300 Paseo Verde Pkwy., Green Valley. 17mi southeast of the Strip via I-15 West to I-215 East; exit on Greek Valley Pkwy.
702-617-7570 or 866-782-9487.
www.greenvalleyranchresort.com.

The Spa at Green Valley Ranch is a lavish destination of its own, encompassing a separate salon building, a private lap and sun-bathing pool overlooking the Las Vegas valley, a fitness center, and a Zen-themed inner chamber with a steam room, sauna, Jacuzzi and dipping pools. A 20,000-square-foot expansion was completed in the summer of 2005, increasing the number of private treatment rooms from 12 to 28. Eight of those are located below ground, where the glass bottom of the reflecting pool in front of the spa forms a ceiling of filtered sunlight through the water above. Don't miss the Eminence Paprika signature facial, an invigorating 80-minute herb facial using Hungarian paprika, wild plum and apricot purée to stimulate the skin.

The Spa at Wynn Las Vegas

3131 Las Vegas Blvd. S.
702-770-7000 or 888-320-7123.
www.wynnlasvegas.com.

In addition to nearly 50 treatment rooms, the Spa offers a spacious Jacuzzi flanked by cool plunge pools, two "deluge" chambers where powerful water columns pound out sore muscles on tired shoulder and neck areas; a waiting area by a fire that seems to spring from a flood of glistening rock

The Spa at Wynn Las Vegas

Wynn Las Vegas

crystals and a large coed waiting room/Zen chamber between the men's and women's area paneled in faux Indian carved stone, with soothing fountains amid stands of bamboo. Some unusual offerings for treatments here include the Arabian Massage, an 80-minute session of warm oils massaged into powerful pressure point areas in the scalp and feet, as well as an all-over body massage.

🛁 The Spa at Trump

702-982-0000 or 877-878-6711.
www.trumplasvegashotel.com.

Although this spa is not bathed in gold, it infuses jewels into every touch. The Spa at Trump is the only spa on The Strip so far to use Shiffa, a product line out of Dubai that infuses precious oils with the powers of diamonds, emeralds, rubies and sapphires. Clients choose their stone according to their desired state: diamonds for clarity and enlightenment;

Emeralds for harmony; Rubies for revitalization and Emeralds for healing and intuition. Facsimiles of the stones are placed about the room and the therapist then rubs elixirs paired with the gem of choice into the client's skin with a deep, heated massage.

Another first for Vegas –guests will find the city's only Kate Somerville facials available there, in fact the only spot you can currently find them outside of West Hollywood. Meticulously trained therapists consult with patients and then produce the secrets that have hooked a Hollywood following. Among the options—an intensified LED light that beams deep into cells to produce healthy collagens. The healing element of The Spa at Trump continues in the relaxation room with teas and healthy snacks (antioxidant gummy bears anyone?) and spritzes from Sprayology, which uses homeopathic principles to calm, rejuvenate, fix travel stress and even combat hot flashes. Helpful "spa attaches" assist with any need, from blending teas to preparing iPod selections. Beauty services extend beyond nails and hair to 15-minute teeth whitening, even shaving. Men can have a full shaving session using Bali-based Hommage herbal products. Healthy cuisine is available at H2(eau) overlooking the pool area. Choose power smoothies and elixirs for a meal in a drink. A quiet lap pool for soaking and sunning is just outside and makes a good place to rest after a treatment, or for a peaceful lunch. The pool is heated for year round use.

Drift Spa at Palms

4381 W. Flamingo Rd.
702-932-7777 or 866-942-7772.
www.palmsplace.com.

Drift Spa at Palms puts a 50,000-square-foot, two-story, sanctuary of sunlight and design in the Palms new 50-story glass tower just off The Strip. The spa brings Las Vegas's first true "hammam," a coed Turkish bath, that is traditionally a place to detox and relax while catching up on the local gossip. If the desert sun doesn't do the job, guests can bronze up in the spa's Sunset Tan wing and complete their 'E!" moment with a color-up in Michael Boychuck's salon. There's a spa access fee of $30 for hotel guests and $35 for non-guests that can be waived with such treatments as the "Rockin' Desert Quench," an 80-minute time-stopper that starts with envelopment in warmed agave nectar, followed by a desert body buff made from crushed desert plants and flowers, a massage with warmed basalt stones, and then a desert aloe wrap, topped with desert flowers body butter.

Hammam, Drift Spa at Palms

Palms Place Hotel & Spa

Spa at Red Rock Resort

11011 W. Charleston Blvd.
702-797-7777 or 866-767-7773.
www.redrocklasvegas.com.

Guests can plan an entire vacation around this spa, a resort destination, 20 minutes west of The Strip. Ultra-modern design inspired by the surrounding Red Rock Canyon keeps the spa drenched in rich shades of red with accents of cream and chocolate brown. Adventure Spa, the first of its kind in Vegas, combines the spa experience with the beauty of nature by packaging pampering with desert adventures. A secluded pool area adds sanctuary and soaking to this high desert escape. If the city is not electric enough for you, amp up with an Espresso Scrub or Espresso Anti-cellulite Wrap. Or take it down a notch with a professional Reiki session.

Well Spa at Platinum

211 E. Flamingo Rd.
702-365-5000 or 877-211-9211.
www.theplatinumhotel.com.

The Platinum's tony and compact Well Spa offers a swell of soft blue and green hues to soothe and comfort and plenty of corners and cubbies within which to retreat between treatments. Especially lovely are chaises surrounded bordered by gossamer veils for privacy, with blankets, teas and fruits within reach. Couples can reconnect through a Pittura Festa where they can paint one another with colorful mud, relax in a private steam room and enjoy a Swiss shower before melting into side-by-side massages.

SPAS

RESTAURANTS

The venues listed below were selected for their ambience, location and/or value for money. Rates indicate the average cost of an appetizer, a main and a dessert for one person (not including tax, gratuity or beverages). Most restaurants are open daily and accept major credit cards. Call for information regarding reservations, dress code and opening hours. For a list of restaurants by theme, see p151. The Michelin Guide (pp152–155) has more recommended restaurants.

| Luxury | **$$$$** | over $100 | Moderate | **$$** | $25–$50 |
| Expensive | **$$$** | $50–$100 | Inexpensive | **$** | under $25 |

LUXURY

Alize

$$$$ **French**
The Palms. 4321 W. Flamingo Rd. Dinner only. 702-951-7000. www.andrelv.com.

You can come for the views—the top floor of the Palms offers all the twinkling and blinking entertainment you could want—or come for the menu that André Rochat has prepared. The recipient of a star this year from Michelin testers, Rochat offers savory French favorites in his foie gras and escargot presentations and adds those accents to Pan Seared Muscovy Duck Breast, Pork Tenderloin, even Peppercorn Crusted filet Mignon with Cognac cream sauce.

Aureole

$$$$ **Contemporary American**
Mandalay Bay, 3950 Las Vegas Blvd. S. Dinner only. 702-632-9325, or 800-632-7000. www.aureolelv.com.

Celebrated chef Charlie Palmer brought his New York City restaurant to town in 1999 and it continues to win accolades for both its culinary combinations and wine pairings. Centerpiece of these sprawling, whitewashed and wood interiors is the four-story, stainless-steel and glass wine tower was designed by Adam Tihany. "Wine angels," aerialists/wine stewards, will retrieve your preferred vintage among the 10,000 bottles by means of mechanical hoists. The menu ranges from succulent citrus-grilled escolar to a hearty caramelized veal chop. Charlie's Onion Soup is a fixture with foie gras, truffles and a Gruyere pastry puff. Prix-fixe, three-course tasting menus start at $75, with wine pairings added for $55.

Binion's Steak House

$$$$ **Surf & Turf**
128 Fremont St. (in Binion's Gambling Hall and Hotel). Dinner only. 702-382-1600. www.binions.com.

This is true old school Vegas, but with a view. Tuxed waiters serve seafood and prime rib on candlelit tables high above the city (24 floors, but that was a high rise in mid-century Las Vegas). A pianist adds to the retro romance on weekends. The signature plate is chicken fried lobster, if you dare.

Bradley Ogden

$$$$ Californian
Caesars Palace, 3570 Las Vegas Blvd. S. Dinner only. 702-731-7413, or 877-346-4642. www.caesars.com.

San Francisco chef Bradley Ogden's signature Las Vegas restaurant is an eye-catcher, right off the lobby of Caesars Palace. Ogden, who gained fame for his culinary creations at the Lark Creek Inn in Marin County, California, creates a new menu daily according to the best seasonal ingredients he can muster. Fresh seems to be the theme of the restaurant and complements the sleek design. Maytag blue cheese soufflé, Columbia River wild King salmon, and Four Story Farms dry-aged ribeye are just a sampling of what you might find. Want something more casual, less time-consuming and less expensive? Sit at the bar and grab a lighter menu featuring the likes of raw oysters, sandwiches and artisan cheeses.

Hank's Fine Steaks

$$$$ Prime Cuts
2300 Paseo Verde Pkwy., Henderson (at Green Valley Ranch Resort). 702-617-7515. www.sanpietro.net.

Bring your appetite and your wallet. Australian lobster tail here sells in multiple pounds, if you want it. There are all the traditional Vegas victuals here: aged and mesquite broiled meats big enough for basketball players, retro sides like mac 'n cheese and tater tots, and all sorts of sauces. And it's all served beneath crystal chandeliers and complemented by an ample martini menu. A pianist performs nightly.

Le Cirque

$$$$ French
Bellagio. 3600 Las Vegas Blvd. S. Dinner only. 702-693-7111. www.bellagio.com.

Straight from the Maccioni family of New York, Le Cirque has made quite the sensation in Las Vegas and recently earned a Michelin star for its exquisite, bold, transcendent persona. The room is as exciting as the food here—colorful whimsy designed by Adam D. Tihany. Count on creative fusion preparations with French accents such as Szechwan Pepper and Cardamom Roasted Salmon, Confit Vegetables, Lobster Oil, Crustacean Jus; Rabbit Symphony: Ravioli, Roasted Loin, Braised Leg with Crispy Spaëtzles, Riesling Sauce; Save room for pastry chef Jaret Blinn's desserts.

Restaurant Guy Savoy

$$$$ French Californian
Caesars Palace. 3570 Las Vegas Blvd. S. 702-731-7286. Dinner only. www.guysavoy.com.

Guy Savoy, inventive kitchen maestro of three-Michelin-star fame in Paris, earned two more in Las Vegas in 2008 from for his statements using unsung American ingredients, such as Santa Barbara prawns, Hawaiian pomfret and Long Island oysters and putting them to work with deft simplicity. Find such hits as artichoke and black truffle soup; cardamom duck stuffed with foie gras and glazed chestnuts; and crispy veal sweetbread sandwiches with small potatoes and black truffles. A "TGV" (named for the French bullet train), 90-minute, four-course taste of Savoy experience runs $190 per person with an added wine program recommendable and at the ready. The $290 per person, ten-course "menu prestige" option makes it a whole evening.

EXPENSIVE

Ceres

$$$ **American**
221 N. Rampart Blvd. (at JW Marriott). Phone: 702-869-7381. www.jwlasvegasresort.com.

Ceres produces creative American cuisine in comfortable surroundings allowing for quiet conversation, calm, and comely aesthetics. Floor-to-ceiling windows let in the light and look out onto lush gardens and the Spring Mountains beyond. The menu produces such starters as crab fondue in Mornay sauce and poached Aussie prawns while entrees include pan-seared John Dory in coconut lemongrass, and exotic mushroom risotto.

CUT

$$$ **Steakhouse**
Palazzo, 3325 Las Vegas Blvd S. 702-789-4141. www.palazzo lasvegas.com/cut.aspx.

The 160-seat cruelty-free CUT steakhouse at Palazzo shows its stars through a menu of organically grown ingredients, coddled farm animals and a sustainable food approach from seed to feed to earth-friendly menus. Combining Wolfgang Puck's kitchen wisdom and passion for culinary perfection, CUT earns its chops as possibly the finest steakhouse in Vegas, even if you don't eat steak. The corn-fed, Nebraska-raised and

35-day dry-aged USDA prime cuts, the Japanese Wagyu wedges, and the Kobe short ribs will just about lay you flat on taste alone, but the Lobster & Crab "Louis" Cocktail with Spicy Tomato-Horseradish, and Roasted Wild French Turbot choices could steal the show.

Daniel Boulud Brasserie

$$$ **French**
Wynn Las Vegas, 3131 Las Vegas Blvd. S. Dinner only. 702-770-7000 or 702-770-3463. www.wynnlasvegas.com.

Daniel Boulud's culinary empire has come to include a lakeside spot at Wynn Las Vegas—a good vantage point from which to watch the light and sound spectacles that reign over the lake nightly.
Considered a place for casual dining, the room sports a modern look with French-country accents; outside you'll find a comely garden terrace. Moules frites, duck confit and organic chicken grand-mère share menu space with grilled salmon and porterhouse for two. The Michelin star chef's signature DB Burger (ground beef stuffed with braised short ribs, foie gras and black truffles) also appears on the brasserie menu.

Fleur de Lys

$$$ **Contemporary French**
Mandalay Bay, 3950 Las Vegas Blvd. S. Dinner only. 702-632-9400. www.mandalaybay.com.

San Francisco chef Hubert Keller has made his Las Vegas debut at this chic establishment at Mandalay Bay. Fleur de Lys has a formal atmosphere with three prix-fixe menu options that that provide ample opportunity to showcase Keller's innovative fare. The chef spices up his French culinary training with accents from California and the American Southwest. Much-ordered entrées include Hawaiian swordfish with tomato poivrade, fennel rouille, mussels and bouillabaisse jus; and roasted squab breast stuffed with foie gras and truffles.

Hugo's Cellar

$$$ Steakhouse
202 Fremont St. (in the Four Queens). 702-385-4011. Dinner only. www.hugoscellar.com.

Voted as Best Gourmet Room in Las Vegas for five years running, this was *the* place in town when it opened in the mid-1960s. And it is still as elegant as it was then, presenting each female guest with a long-stemmed rosebud and bringing out the "cart" when it comes to its customized Caesar salads. Following your filet leave room for the desserts flambé, also served tableside.

Mesa Grill

$$$ Southwestern
Caesars Palace, 3570 S. Las Vegas Blvd. S. 702-650-5965 or 800-634-6661. www.mesagrill.com.

Celebrity chef Bobby Flay's first restaurant outside New York City, Mesa Grill is located in the Augustus Tower at Caesars Palace, where it earned its first Michelin star. Here, Flay interprets zesty Southwestern cuisine in a high-energy dining room.

MESA Grill at Caesars Palace
Brian Jones

Between his three New York City restaurants—including the original Mesa Grill—cookbooks, and several shows on the Food TV network, Flay has established himself as a major American culinary force. For Mesa starters, try the smoked chicken and black bean quesadilla or the goat cheese queso fundido. Then perhaps move on to the coffee-spice-rubbed rotisserie filet mignon, or the blue-corn-crusted red snapper. Flay also has restaurants in the Bahamas, Atlantic City and New Jersey.

Michael Mina

$$$ Seafood
Bellagio. 3600 Las Vegas Blvd. S. Dinner only. 702-693-7223. www.bellagio.com.

This is one of four restaurants by Michael Mina in Las Vegas but the only one of his venues to earn the coveted Michelin star. Favorites here include the lobster pot pie, the black mussel soufflé, phyllo crumb-crusted Dover sole and the caviar parfait. The setting is upscale business, lots of woods amid glass and leather in a hectic, but well orchestrated, dining space.

miX, dining room

©miX

 miX

$$$ **French**
THEhotel at Mandalay Bay,
3950 Las Vegas Blvd. S.
Dinner only. 702-632-9500.
www.chinagrillmgt.com.

If Las Vegas is a city of lights, dinner at the one Michelin star Mix is indeed a sparkling date, under the glow of the chandelier's 15,000 hand-blown orbs. Here, on the 64th floor of THEhotel, Alain Ducasse's singular dining venture in Vegas sizzles amid a sleek atmosphere of pearly tones and window walls affording spectacular views of The Strip. The acclaimed chef spares no calories to get his customers' approval. Black truffles and foie gras pair well with many dishes, including pressed chicken and beef tenderloin.
Ducasse's version of that comfort-food staple, macaroni and cheese, is made with ham, Gruyère and black truffles. Before or after dinner, head to the bar for some heady views. Even the bathroom offers a window on this world. The open-air terrace puts you in the clouds.

Nobhill

$$$ **Regional American**
MGM Grand, 3799 Las Vegas
Blvd. S. Dinner only. 702-891-7433.
www.mgmgrand.com.

Inspired by the traditional neighborhood restaurants found throughout the San Francisco area, Chef Michael Mina has combined that city's most innovative dishes into a unique menu. The dining room centers on a wood-fired bread oven. Signature dishes such as lobster pot pie and North Beach cioppino are complemented by organic vegetables and greens.

Rao's

$$$ **Italian**
Caesars Palace. 3570 Las Vegas
Blvd S. No lunch. 702-731-RAOS.
www.raos.com

You can count the cast members of the Sopranos among the signed photos lining the walls at Rao's, a sweet sliver of East Harlem right in the middle of the casino at Caesars Palace. Pasta is served family style with a side of meaty meatballs, the way the 111-year-old original restaurant opposite Jefferson Park on 114th Street always has. Unlike the ten-table New York original you can actually get seated here and get a taste of Frank Pellegrino's legendary chicken with lemon and vinegar, spaghetti with broccoli sauce and seafood salad. No menus are offered. While dining you might be greeted by a member of the Sopranos. The owner, Frank Jr., played the raspy-breathed FBI chief during the series and is the fifth generation of the Rao's family to run the restaurant.

rm seafood

$$$ Seafood
Mandalay Place, 3930 Las Vegas Blvd. S. Dinner only. 702-632-9300. www.rmseafood.com.

Seafood master Rick Moonen closed his acclaimed New York City establishment to put seafood in the desert at **Mandalay Place**, with his vision stamped on every shell and fin. His Las Vegas venture creates a nautical-themed environment of mahogany wood and water, where the freshest of sustainable fish and shellfish make for a succulent dining experience. Whether you choose a tasting

rm seafood

menu with perfectly paired wines or an à la carte selection that changes with the seasons and moods of the kitchen, seafood takes on new character here with such creations as wild striped bass with hen of the woods mushrooms and black truffle vinaigrette; abalone with uni butter and Pacific sturgeon caviar; and Mediterranean mussel soufflé in Madras curry butter.

Rosemary's

$$$ Contemporary American
West Sahara Promenade, 8125 W. Sahara Ave. 702-869-2251. www.rosemarysrestaurant.com.

Rosemary's Restaurant

Rosemary's

Michael and Wendy Jordan are giving the celebrity chefs in Vegas a run for their money with a top-notch gastronomical experience (that's not surprising, since Michael trained under acclaimed New Orleans chef Emeril Lagasse). From sesame seared ahi tuna to grilled veal tenderloin with French lentils and frizzled leeks, everything on the menu is prepared with the utmost attention to detail. Rosie's Goodnight Kiss, a liqueur-spiked after-dinner coffee drink, is guaranteed to give you sweet dreams.

RESTAURANTS

StripSteak

$$$ **American Steak**
Mandalay Bay. 3950 Las Vegas Blvd. S. 702-632-7200. Dinner only. www.mandalaybay.com

StripSteak is what happens when you get a Las Vegas favorite like Michael Mina to open up a not-your-Daddy's steakhouse in one of the hottest hotels in the US. If steak can have a scene, it has one at StripSteak. Catch it on the right night and you might even get hot-pants-clad go-go girls thrown into the meal. Mina makes his mark by infusing the dining scene with technology whether using wood-burning grills or the six circulating, slow-poaching chambers. It's a perfect piece of meat every time, stoked with the subtlest touch of mesquite-infused smokiness. Sides add delicious coronary contraband: fries with dipping sauces, garlic mashed potatoes, tomato-dusted onion rings. Also find true Kumamoto oysters here and Japanese "A5" Kobe steaks.

MODERATE

L'Atelier de Joël Robuchon

$$ **French**
MGM Grand, 3799 Las Vegas Blvd. S. Dinner only. 702-891-7374. www.mgmgrand.com.

Famed Paris chef Joël Robuchon came out of retirement in 2005 to open two new restaurants in Las Vegas. At L'Atelier, located adjacent to MGM Grand's casino, you can appreciate the chef's culinary talents without breaking your budget. Here, 23 seats range along a black granite bar around the open kitchen, where part of

L'Atelier de Joël Robuchon, MGM Grand

Francis George/MGM Mirage

the fun is watching the team of professional chefs prepare your meal. The menu allows diners to mix and match among small plates (seared tuna belly, sautéed foie gras, sardine escabeche) and entrée-size portions (steak tartare, rack of lamb, langoustine fritters). There's also a nine-course tasting menu ($85). Next door, **Joël Robuchon at The Mansion** (*see red tabbed section of this guide*) transports patrons to 1930s France with plush, millennium deux Belle Epoch surroundings and sublime prix-fixe tasting menus that change daily.

The Bootlegger Bistro

$$ **Italian**
7700 Las Vegas Blvd. S., between Warm Springs & Blue Diamond Rds. Open 24 hours. 702-736-4939. www.bootleggerlasvegas.com.

For those who want a touch of Las Vegas the way it used to be, the Bootlegger is for you. Owned by Maria and Albert Perri, and their daughter, Lorraine Hunt (former Lt. Gov of Nevada), this restaurant offers real home-style Italian cooking (Mama Maria comes in three times a week to oversee the making of the sauces, meatballs and sausage) along with great old-fashioned Las Vegas entertainment. On Friday and Saturday nights, Hunt's husband, Blackie, and entertainer Sonny King (Jimmy Durante's partner for 30 years) do a show called Off The Cuff.

Bouchon

$$ French
The Venetian, 3355 Las Vegas Blvd. S. 702-414-6200. www.venetian.com.

Thomas Keller, whose new New York City restaurant, Per Se was recently awarded three Michelin stars, brings his considerable culinary talents to The Venetian at Bouchon. A French pewter bar, a multihued mosaic floor, deep-blue velvet banquettes, antique light fixtures and an expansive hand-painted mural complement the authentic bistro fare here. Breakfast and dinner are served daily; lunch is available on weekends. The seasonal menu offers classics including steak frites, roasted chicken, and trout amandine, bolstered by daily specials. Several items, like croque madame and boudin blanc, are available any time of day.

Brio

$$ Italian
6653 Las Vegas Blvd. S. (in the Las Vegas Town Square Mall). 702-914-9145. www.brioitalian.com.

The thing about this new chain to the Vegas landscape is its location. It's smack in the middle of the new **Town Square Mall**, an open cityscape of decorative small town and European village facades. Brio offers dining and lounging within a spacious outdoor patio

within this setting and even keeps a fire pit going for conversation, ambience and warmth. Find all the flavorful Tuscan-inspired cuisine available under the Nevada sun. Leave room for Tiramisu. Consider brunch here on weekends.

Burger Bar

$$ American
Mandalay Bay, 3930 Las Vegas Blvd. 702-632-9364. www.mandalaybay.com.

Decked out with leatherette booths surrounded by warm woods, Hubert Keller's (of Fleur de Lys) hip Burger Bar at **Mandalay Place** has received much attention for serving the most expensive burger in Las Vegas. The Rossini, for $60, is all Kobe beef, sautéed foie gras and shaved truffles with Madeira sauce, served on an onion bun. But you can build your own more affordable burger (of beef, lamb, turkey or vegetarian) at this upscale eatery for as little as $8. Choose among more than three dozen toppings-from baby spinach and avocado to Jalapeño bacon and foie gras-for an extra 50¢ to $12. Wash down your meal with a selection from the menu of hand-crafted micro-brews.

Japonais

$$ Japanese Fusion
Mirage, 3400 Las Vegas Blvd., S. 702-791-7111. www.japonaisla vegas.com.

The eye-candy interiors by Jeffery Beers are worth the visit alone. But the hot marriage of classic French culinary with precision Japanese preparation begets a dining experience to dazzle the senses with each new creative twist. Try Chestnut Chicken, Le Quack Japonais, or "The Rock," thinly sliced marinated New York strip cooked on a hot rock right at the table.

Louis's Las Vegas

$$ Southern
6559 Las Vegas Blvd. (in the Town Square Mall). 702-202-2400. www.louislasvegas.com.

New Orleans is alive and well at this corner of the 🚋**Town Square Mall** in Las Vegas. The food at both Louis's Las Vegas and Louis's Fish Camp is described as "down home" and that's fine with Chef Louis Osteen, who was named James Beard's "American Express Best Chef Southeast" in 2004. Louis's is the fine dining setting for Crab and Lobster Cakes or Chicken-Fried Duck Breast with spiced pecans. Dine al fresco on the balcony overlooking the streets of the mall. Nearby, Louis's Fish Camp is for casual fare, fun and Bayou beats on the weekends. All can be washed down with a pick from more than 100 labels of Bourbon (in fact, this is the only place in Vegas that offers bourbon lockers for serious sippers).

Mon Ami Gabi

$$ French
Paris Las Vegas, 3655 Las Vegas Blvd. S. 702-944-4224. www.monamigabilasvegas.com.

Named for chef Gambino Soletino, this restaurant offers a charming bistro décor that spells 19th-century Paris all the way. Its patio

Mon Ami Gabi

dining on The Strip (complete with misters to cool patrons in summer) is one of the best people-watching sites in the city, and a great spot from which to view the Bellagio fountain show. At night, the setting turns romantic with candlelight and bistro classics such as steak frites.

Sushi Roku

$$ Japanese
3500 Las Vegas Blvd., S. 702-733-7373. www.sushiroku.com.

This is sushi with a scene, both inside and out. Located in the far reaches of the 🚋**Forum Shops** at Caesars, the restaurant features floor-to-ceiling cathedral-sized windows right over some of the most flamboyant neon on The Strip.

The place is often in use for bachelor (and bachelorette) parties. Try the Omakasi menu of chef's choice plates. Expect usual dishes to have special touches—yellowtail sashimi with diced chilies, or homemade tofu with white truffles or caviar and lemon.

The Restaurant at Platinum

$$ **Creative American**
Platinum Hotel, 11 E. Flamingo Rd.
702-365-5000 or 877-211-9211.
www.theplatinumhotel.com.

The Restaurant's chef Brenton Hammer works with seasonal ingredients to come up with such creative combinations as Butterfish with vanilla-poached gooseberries, smoked almonds, sunchoke, and black lentils; and South Dakota bison encased in a paper-thin layer of crunchy caramel, accompanied by olive "caviar." Prices here run from Strip high to the best deal in town. For instance, a ground Wyagu Kobe sirloin burger will cost \$17, not \$60 *(see Burger Bar)*, and that even includes fries. The chef likes to describe it as 'edgy American meets urban oasis'.

r bar

$$ **Seafood**
Mandalay Place, 3930 Las Vegas
Blvd. S. 702-632-9300.
www.mandalayplace.com.

Sister to rm seafood, r bar occupies part of the same floor. It's located on the ground floor (rm seafood fills the second floor), just off the entrance of **Mandalay Place**, as you're coming from the casino. Eat at the stainless-steel bar, in the high-ceilinged dining room, or on the indoor patio. Pressed for time? Order you meal to-go and head for the pool, your room or wherever. r bar is renowned for its seafood chowders; if you prefer oysters, an oyster-tasting menu offers bivalves fresh from 11 different areas of the Atlantic and Pacific. Chef Rick Moonen practices conscious cuisine, using only caught fish that have a sustainable presence in our oceans, for properly farmed fish and other proteins.

Shibuya

$$ **Japanese**
MGM Grand, 3799 Las Vegas Blvd.
S. Dinner only. 702-891-1111.
www.mgmgrand.com.

Las Vegas News Bureau/LVCVA

Shibuya

The food at Shibuya matches the vibrant urban Tokyo neighborhood from which the restaurant takes its name. The space is divided into three areas that feature sushi, Teppan and à la carte specialties. Complement your entrée with the perfect sake, thanks to Shibuya's sake-pairing program. The room's design captures the essence of fast-paced Tokyo with video screens reflected in mirrored plexiglass above, for a kaleidoscopic effect of constant movement. Master sushi chef Hidebumi Sueyoshi presides over the 50ft marble sushi bar.

Simon Kitchen & Bar

$$ Contemporary American
Hard Rock Hotel, 4455 Paradise Rd. Dinner only. 702-693-4440.

Kerry Simon's 21st-century take on American food contrasts with the distinctly Asian décor of this hot-for-now 140-seat restaurant. Although the Gen-X crowd here is often celebrity-packed (Mick Jagger, Paul McCartney and Goldie Hawn number among past diners) the food is what really attracts attention. The chef's playful interpretations range from chicken curry presented in a white take-out container to "topless" apple pie or chocolate-chunk cookies and milk. At the end of the meal, Simon's signature, a fluffy bowlful of pink cotton candy, is presented to each table.

Vintner Grill, West Las Vegas

**$$ California/
Mediterranean Fusion**
10100 W. Charleston Blvd., Suite 150. 702-214-5590. www.vglasvegas.com.

Ok. Madonna dined here. So did Jagger, McCartney, Springstein, Leno, Streisand, the list goes on. Located in a stripmall business park in Summerlin, some ten miles west of the neon near the JW Marriott and Red Rock Resort, Vintner Grill still packs the Viceroy-style, retro-chic dining room most nights. Chef Matthew Silverman cut his teeth in the kitchens of Wolfgang Puck and by 30 managed to make his mark on the competitive Las Vegas culinary scene with an American-Mediterranean fusion approach that yields such original entrées as crispy cala-

mari with haricot verts, lemon and curry aioli; bistro steak medallions with basmati rice and portabella mushroom cream; and Moroccan-spiced lamb spare ribs with apricot glaze—hints of black truffle fungi always in the background.

White Chocolate Grill

$$ American
9510 S. Eastern Ave., Henderson. 702-436-7100. whitechocolategrill.com.

Here, you can have your chocolate and eat it too. In fact chocolate offerings take top place on the menu, even before starters. Still, you'll want to have dinner first, in the form of classic American fare: Southern fried chicken salad, blackened mahi, all manner of burgers and sandwiches. Besides forbidden sweets the restaurant serves up flavorful wood-fired entrees amid walls of artworks and warm wood designs.

INEXPENSIVE

Canyon Ranch Café

$$ Contemporary American
The Venetian, 3355 Las Vegas Blvd. S. No dinner. 702-414-3633. www.venetian.com.

Who says you can't eat lean in Las Vegas? At Canyon Ranch Café you'll find truly fat-defying nour-ishment. A member of the famed Tucson spa family, the signature café was created by some of the most talented spa chefs and nutritionists in the nation. Enjoy pancakes with ginger-maple syrup, vegetarian stir-fry and a horserad-ish salmon sandwich with cranberry ketchup; all without guilt. In case you're counting, the menu lists the calorie, protein and carb counts for all dishes. The café is located off the open lobby of the **Canyon Ranch SpaClub** *(see Spas).*

Chin Chin

$ Chinese
New York-New York, 3790 Las Vegas Blvd. S. 702-740-6300.
www.newyorknewyorkcasino.com.

True to its name, which means "to your health," this California chain offers "lite" dishes-prepared with little or no oil-and uses no MSG in its food. You can watch chefs in the open exhibition kitchen whip up tasty dim sum appetizers like shredded chicken salad with red ginger dressing, and Anthony's Special Noodles (lo mein with chicken in a spicy cilantro sauce).

Pho

$ Vietnamese
Treasure Island. 3300 Las Vegas Blvd. S. 702-894-7111.

Tucked inside The Coffee Shop at Treasure Island, Pho is an unexpected delight and marks the only Vietnamese restaurant on The Strip. It only offers 30 seats and is a great place to catch an inexpensive meal that can be had in a hurry. Find signature Vietnamese favorites, most contained within the Pho, a base of a rich broth with vermicelli noodles, soy and fish spices and fresh herbs. The main rice and meat dishes flow to the curries, although there is a savory selection for vegans as well. Don't miss the Vietnamese-style egg rolls that use fresh lemon grass and mint wrapped in a rubbery rice dough, and dipped in sweet and tangy chili sauce. Most meals run at around $7.

'Wichcraft

$ American
MGM Grand, 3799 Las Vegas Blvd., S. 702-891-1111 or 702-891-3166.
www.mgmgrand.com.

Award-winning chef Tom Colicchio has brought an offshoot of his New York City sandwich shop to town, serving breakfast and lunch from 10am–6pm. Don't miss Colicchio's signature house-roasted pork loin sandwich served warm with red cabbage and jalapenos on ciabatta bread, or his Sicilian tuna with fennel, black olives and lemon confit stuffed in a crusty baguette. Breakfast sandwiches, available all day, include skirt steak with fried eggs and oyster mushrooms on a ciabatta roll, and prosciutto with sweet butter on a baguette.

BLT Burger

$ American Diner
Mirage, 3400 Las Vegas Blvd., S. 702-792-7888.
www.bltburger.com.

You don't have to be pregnant to love the fried pickles here. Chef Laurent Tourondel delivers sinful food to Sin City. You cannot get further from your "good and should" list than milk shakes 14 ways with, or without, added kick; fries six ways including jalapeno poppers and flat waffle bites; and seven styles of burgers with or without the bun. The I'll-diet-tomorrow dessert choices include S'mores and "Krispy Kreme" Doughnut Bread Pudding.

BUFFETS

The search for the ultimate buffet is sport in Las Vegas, where rather than stars, buffets should be rated in the number of plates stacked at a setting. The free "chuckwagon" days of old may be over and the price of admission to these divine dining chambers is not always cheap, but it is always a bargain. A few quick tips for avoiding the buffet lines: go at off times if you can: dine before 6:30pm or after 8pm for instance. Join a player's club, play a few rounds of slots and get a free buffet voucher. It usually includes a line pass or a place in the "VIP" queue. Choose a top price buffet. The food is well worth the tariff, the service is on the money, the room is spacious and quiet, and lines are short.

Bellagio serves venison, duck breast, steamed clams and king crab legs in addition to the usual buffet fare *(702-693-1111; www. bellagiolasvegas.com; $ breakfast; $$ lunch & dinner)*.

Carnival World Buffet at the Rio features a moderately priced Mongolian grill where you can pick your own ingredients and have them cooked with chicken, beef or shrimp *(702-252-7777; www.playrio.com; $)*.

Cravings at the Mirage is a recent redo on the Las Vegas buffet scene with special attention paid to service and design such as food stations where dishes are cooked to order. The dim sum station is particularly popular. Cravings is in the mid-priced tier *(702-791-1111; www.mirage.com; $ breakfast, $$ lunch & dinner)*.

The Buffet at TI takes the less-is-more approach and offers better quality food but less choice than might be available elsewhere. Five food stations, Asian, Italian, barbeque, salads and desserts, offer selections such as dim sum, sushi, Korean hot pots, osso buco, barbecued ribs, and rotisserie chicken Cordon Blue. The price is mid-tier for an excellent presentation *(702-894-7111; www.treasureisland.com; $$ breakfast, lunch & dinner)*.

The Flamingo's Paradise Garden Buffet has a view of the Wildlife Habitat and a prime rib, shrimp and crab buffet every night. The buffet ranks high among the lower-priced Strip buffet choices *(702-733-3111; www. flamingolasvegas.com; $ breakfast & brunch, dinner)*.

Main Street Station's Garden Court Buffet has great prices and terrific food *(702-387-1896; www. boydgaming.com; $ breakfast, lunch & dinner; kids under 3 eat free)*.

Le Village Buffet at Paris Las Vegas offers food stations from various French provinces, as well as an incredible assortment of pas-

---

The Un-Buffet

Held each Sunday at Bally's Steakhouse, Bally's Sterling Brunch *(702-967-7999; www.ballyslv.com; $$$)* is not a buffet in the traditional sense. The menu changes weekly, but you can always expect sturgeon caviar, Cordon Rouge champagne, fresh sushi, made-to-order omelets, oysters, beef tenderloin, lobster and hovering white-gloved waiters to cater to your concerns. A true Vegas hold-out from the glorious gourmet room days.

tries, and crêpes cooked to order *(702-946-7000; www.parislv.com; $ breakfast, $$ lunch & dinner).*

The Spice Market Buffet is possibly one of the best buffets in town, revered by locals and visitors alike. Find aromatic specialties here such as tandoori chicken and Middle Eastern salads, fresh hot and cold crabs legs, a wok station that does not overcook and over saturate the contents, a Mongolian barbeque, even cherries jubilee inside a copious dessert bar *(702-785-5555; www.planethollywood.com; $ breakfast & lunch, $$ dinner).*

The Feast Buffets at Station Casino Resorts are a local's secret in Las Vegas. The prices are right, the selections run from common to haute, the desserts are plentiful and creative and there are always a mix of ethnic tasting stations, from Mongolian grill to Mexican to prime rib. Find Feast Buffets at Green Valley Ranch *(702-617-7777)*, Sunset Station *(702-547-7777)*, Boulder Station *(702-432-7777)*, Palace Station *(702-367-2411)*, Santa Fe Station *(702-658-4900)*, Texas Station *(702-631-1000)*, and Red Rock Casino Resort *(702-797-7777; www.stationcasinos.com; $ breakfast, lunch, dinner).* Red Rock's Feast is especially popular for its Sunday Champagne Brunch from 8am–4pm.

House of Blues Sunday Gospel Brunch is not quite the most expensive buffet in town but certainly the most entertaining, House of Blues Sunday Gospel Brunch is a must for the cornbread and coffee crowd who want some spirit with those eggs. Both the 10am and 1pm seatings bring bottomless mimosas to wash down hickory -smoked bacon, cheese-laced grits, and bourbon-soaked ham, all the belting sound you can handle. *(Mandalay Bay; 702-632-7600; www.hob.com/venues/clubvenues/lasvegas/gospelbrunch.asp; $$).*

The Village Seafood Buffet at Rio is the city's only true seafood buffet. If you want seafood some two hundred ways, this is the right place. Chef Richard Leggett who hails from the Ritz-Carlton in Buckhead, GA, is quick to point out 84 hot food dishes on the line, as well as 96 cold dishes (including salads and sushis) and, well, 51 desserts. The buffet re-opened in March 2008 after a $12 million, four-month hiatus to do a total design revamp and make the cool, upscale décor match the $38 per person admission *(open daily for dinner only).* Now there is a wine bar with selections from California, Washington and New Zealand, a VIP section, and a phalanx of sparkling new stations de cuisine including Crustaceans, Raw, Mediterranean, American Coastal, Pacific Rim, Baja, Sushi and Sashimi, Salad, and the Turf part of the surf.

It all amounts to some 750,000 pounds of seafood a month cooked in small pans to keep every presentation fresh. Try the tiny Asian lobster tails available each night, as are such faves as paella and cioppino. Desserts are about cupcakes, gelato and chocolate chip bread pudding.

There is also a flambé of the day for those who save room. *(Rio, 702-252-7777; www.riolasvegas.com; $$).*

RESTAURANTS BY THEME

Looking for the best meal deal in town? Want to dine where the glitterati go? Need the right place for that special occasion? Las Vegas is fast becoming a culinary capital of the world's top chefs, and that means abundant competition for your dining dollar. In the preceding pages, we've organized restaurants by price category, so here we've broken them out by theme to help you plan just the right evening out.

Alfresco Dining
Daniel Boulud Brasserie (p 130)
Bouchon (p 135)
Mon Ami Gabi (p 136)
Vintner Grill (p 138)

Best Bang for the Buck
Burger Bar (p 135)
Canyon Ranch Café (p 138)
Chin Chin (p 139)
Pho (p 139)
r bar (p 137)
The Restaurant at Platinum (p 137)
'wichcraft (p 139)
L'Atelier de Joël Robuchon (p 134)

Celebrity Chefs
Alize (Andre Rochat) (p 128)
Aureole (Charlie Palmer) (p 128)
Bradley Ogden (p 129)
Le Cirque (Sirio Maccioni) (p 129)
Daniel Boulud
Brasserie (p 130)
Fleur de Lys (Hubert Keller) (p 130)
L'Atelier de
Joël Robuchon (p 134)
Mesa Grill (Bobby Flay) (p 131)
Michael Mina (Michael Mina) (p 131)
Mix (Alain Ducasse) (p 132)
Restaurant Guy Savoy
(Guy Savoy) (p 129)
rm seafood (Rick Moonen) (p 133)
Simon Kitchen & Bar
(Kerry Simon) (p 138)
Strip Steak (Michael Mina) (p 134)

Dinner with a View
Alize (p 128)
miX (p 132)
Sushi Roku (p 136)

Eating with Kids
BLT Burger (p 139)
Burger Bar (p 135)
Mon Ami Gabi (p 136)
r bar (p 137)
'wichcraft (p 139)

Hip Haunts
Aureole (p 128)
Bradley Ogden (p 129)
Daniel Boulud Brasserie (p 130)
miX (p 132)
Shibuya (p 137)
Simon Kitchen & Bar (p 138)
StripSteak (p 134)
Sushi Roku (136)

Pre-show Dinner
L'Atelier de Robuchon (p 134)
Le Cirque (p 129)
Daniel Boulud Brasserie (p 130)
Michael Mina (p 131)
Nobhill (p 132)
Pho (p 139)
r bar (p 137)
Rao's (p 132)
Shibuya (p 137)
Simon Kitchen & Bar (p 138)
StripSteak (p 134)

Shop and Dine
Brio (p 135)
Burger Bar (p 135)
r bar (p 137)
rm seafood (p 133)

Special-Occasion Restaurants
Alize (p 128)
Aureole (p 128)
Bradley Ogden (p 129)

Fleur de Lys, Mandalay Bay

MGM Mirage

RESTAURANTS

143

HOTELS

The properties listed below were selected for their ambience, location and value for money. Prices reflect the average cost for a standard double room for two people (not including applicable taxes, including the city's 7.25% hotel tax). Hotels in Las Vegas constantly offer special discount rates. Properties are located in Las Vegas, unless otherwise specified. For a listing of additional casino hotels, see Casinos. See the end of this section for a list of hotels by theme. The Michelin Guide (*pp152–155*) has more recommended hotels.

Luxury	$$$$$	over $350		Moderate	$$$	$175-$250
Expensive	$$$$	$250-$350		Inexpensive	$ –$$	$100-$175

LUXURY

Four Seasons Hotel Las Vegas

$$$$$ 424 Rooms
3960 Las Vegas Blvd. S.
702-632-5000 or 877-632-5000.
www.fourseasons.com.

The only hotel on The Strip without a casino, Four Seasons maintains its distinctive identity even though its rooms occupy the 36th to 39th floors of adjoining Mandalay Bay. Spacious rooms are done in wood and rattan with floor-to-ceiling windows looking out on the mountains and desert. For a memorable dining experience, try the artisan-aged beef at **Charlie Palmer Steak ($$$)**.

EXPENSIVE

Hard Rock Hotel

$$$$ 657 Rooms
4455 Paradise Rd.
702-693-5000 or 800-693-7625.
www.hardrockhotel.com.

You know from the moment that you see the chandelier with 32 gold saxophones hanging from it that you're in the Hard Rock Hotel. Set off The Strip (at Harmon Ave.), this 11-story property features a casino decorated with memorabilia from past and present rock stars. Many of the latter perform in the hotel's 1,200-seat theater. Sleek rooms sport a musical motif with leather headboards and French doors. Of course, there's a Hard Rock Café on-site, and **Nobu ($$)** serves the acclaimed Japanese cuisine of chef Nobu Matsuhisa.

The Ritz-Carlton Lake Las Vegas

$$$$ 349 Rooms
1610 Lake Las Vegas Pkwy.,
Henderson. 702-567-4700 or 800-241-3333. www.ritz-carlton.com.

Nestled on the shores of the largest privately owned **lake** in the US, this golf and spa resort evokes Mediterranean waterside villages with its clay-tile roofs and arched doorways, and wraps guests in luxury with marble baths and Frette linens. Treat yourself to a day at the Italian-inspired Spa Vita di Lago.

Skylofts at MGM Grand

$$$$ 51 Loft Suites
3799 Las Vegas Blvd., S. 877-646 638. www.skylotsmgmgrand.com.

The 51 super-luxe lofts in the MGM Grand penthouse are actually a hotel within a hotel with their own elevator entrance, check-in desk and concierge. Anyone with a grand or (a lot) more to spend on a night in neon heaven above The Strip can have it all in a town that does it all, no holds barred. The 1,400- to 6,000-square-foot 1, 2 and 3-bedroom, split-level lofts come with an army of built-ins, such as floor-to-ceiling two-story windows, custom Bang & Olufsen and loaded Sony HDTV audio-visual equipment, espresso machines with custom selection of exclusive coffees (and fine herbal teas); custom-designed radio-controlled remote panels to operate TV, DVD, radio, CD, internet radio, drapes, temperature and lights; high-speed internet access and Anichini and Fili D'Oro linens. This is Vegas a la Georges V or Cipriani, over neon rather than Belle Epoche or Renaissance walkways. Have your Champagne at the bar or in the infinity-edge tub with a "Champagne Bubbles" massaging you amid rotating chromatherapy lights. Sweeter yet, guests can avail themselves of limousine transportation to locations on the Las Vegas Strip while a personal valet unpacks their luggage.

 Trump Las Vegas

$$$$ 1,282 Suites
200 Fashion Show Dr.
702-982-0000 or 866-646-8164
www.trumplasvegashotel.com.

The Trump touch is apparent the minute you step into this new 64-story high-rise along The Strip: an expansive, marble lobby illuminated by crystal chandeliers, no lines at the check-in counter, no intrusions from the sounds of

slots—in fact there is no casino at all here. Trump offers a bit of dignity on The Strip and complements it with non-smoking suites that pack all the comforts of home—even if it is someone else's home. This is a condo-hotel and keeping the owners (and guests) happy is the name of the game. To do that, Trump offers 24-hour room service and concierge service, a full service luxury 🛁 **spa**, a fine dining salon called DJT (with every dish approved by The Don), a calming high tea session in the afternoon and splendid cocktails just before dinner. It's a bit of upper West Side on The Strip, steps away from "Fifth Avenue" shopping at 🛍️ **Fashion Show Mall**.

MODERATE

Bally's Las Vegas

$$$ 3,079 Rooms
3645 Las Vegas Blvd. S.
702-967-4111 or 800-634-3434.
www.ballyslv.com.

Bally's may look a bit worn compared to The Strip's flashier megaresorts, but its attractive 500-square-foot rooms are among the largest in town. Besides the casino, there's a swimming pool, a lovely spa, a salon and a shopping area. Bally's is also the home of the Vegas classic Jubilee! *(see Productions)*.

🏨 **Loews Lake Las Vegas Resort**

$$$ 539 Rooms
101 Montelago Blvd., in Henderson, 702- 567-6000, 877-285-6397

This hotel changed recently from a Hyatt Regency to a Loews, but most of the Moorish décor and the

HOTELS

Rio All-Suite Casino & Hotel

Las Vegas News Bureau/LVCVA

spirit remains the same. Marssa is the signature restaurant now but the spa remains the same and the rooms still sport clean and handsome lines, linens and décor. The property overlooks the 300-acre **Lake Las Vegas** and sits astride an 18-hole champion golf course by Jack Nicklaus.

Meridian Suites

$$$ All-Suites
250 E. Flamingo Rd.
702-990-0634 or 888-654-4227.
www.meridianlasvegas.com.

Accommodations at this property are all suites since Meridian was originally a luxury apartment complex in the 1990s. Today, those quarters are for visitors seeking roomier accommodations with all the built-ins: kitchen, fireplace, separate bedrooms, multiple bathrooms, in a lush and quiet setting not far from The Strip.

Montelago Village Resort, Lake Las Vegas

$$$ 347 Suites
30 Strada di Villaggi, Henderson.
702-564-4700 or 866-564-4799
www.montelagovillage.com

Lake Las Vegas Resort is Las Vegas' answer to a Las Vegas getaway.

The air is clean and clear in this spot 20 miles from the city at the edge of the blue, 300-acre **Lake Las Vegas**. The Montelago Village Resort offers condo-style hotel rooms right by the village, which comes alive on weekends with musical concerts, dine-arounds and art fests.

Rio All-Suite Casino & Hotel

$$$ 2,500 Suites
3700 W. Flamingo Rd.
702-252-7777 or 888-746-7482.
www.playrio.com.

The Rio may be off the beaten track but it's hugely popular, drawing hip young party-goers from The Strip with its three nightclubs: Club Rio, the Voodoo Lounge, and Bikinis. Airy, well-appointed suites feature floor-to-ceiling windows and a separate dressing area, plus a refrigerator and safe. Check out The Village Seafood Buffet. for the best seafood spread in town

Signature at MGM Grand

$$$ 1,695 Suites
145 East Harmon Ave.
702-797-6000 or 877-612-2121
www.signaturemgmgrand.com

The Signature is MGM Grand's answer to solid ground. Three 38-story towers, a partnership between MGM Mirage and the Turnberry Group, connect to MGM by moving walkway, putting all the nightlife, restaurants, entertainment and action of the Resort and The Strip within shouting distance. But the Signature is a bit of a retreat from all that. The suites here are comfortable and efficient, featuring top of the line kitchen appliances, large granite

MUST STAY

bathrooms, often a fireplace and balcony and wide views of the valley. Each property has its own pool if the 6.5-acre Grand pool complex seems like too much. You can also find Starbuck's and other amenities in the lobby. Suites are non-smoking and a good value in Las Vegas for convenience and cost, especially for families.

INEXPENSIVE

Alexis Park Resort & Spa

$ –$$ 500 Suites
375 E. Harmon Ave. between Koval Lane & Paradise Rd. 702-796-3300.
www.alexispark.com.

Set amid winding paths, waterfalls and lush greenery, this resort filled with two-story white stucco villas began life as a complex of town homes. Located a half-mile from The Strip, Alexis Park doesn't have a casino. What it does have are tennis courts, three pools and a spa. Tastefully decorated suites are equipped with refrigerators, mini-bars and VCRs; larger units have vaulted -ceilings, gas fireplaces and whirlpool tubs.

Artisan Hotel

$ –$$ 64 Rooms
1501 W Sahara Ave.,
702-214-4000 or 800-554-4092,
www.theartisanhotel.com

This handsomely decorated boutique hotel is an unusual find for visitors who want to try something other than a megaresort on The Strip. A Mediterranean style provides a smattering of peace with comfortable opium style chaises and shady cabanas. There's a lounge onsite with DJ action

on weekends and a spa is set to open in 2008. All day dining can be found in the Artisan Fine Dining Room and a Champagne brunch on weekends makes for a fancy affair without the fancy prices. The location is good near both The Strip and shopping.

Blue Moon Resort

$ –$$ 45 Suites
2651 Westwood Dr. 2702-361-9099
or 866-798-9194.
www.bluemoonlv.com

Blue Moon is the place to stay if you are gay—and you are a man. It's off-Strip, hidden and private with a killer pool scene. Accommodations are plush and large in desert tones and leathers, with high threadcount linens and flat-screened TVs. The lagoon pool is pimped with a 10-men Jacuzzi grotto covered by a 10-foot waterfall, trunks optional. Complimentary continental breakfast included daily.

Emerald Suites

$ –$$ 396 Suites
9145 Las Vegas Blvd. S.
702-948-9999 or 866-847-2002.
www.emeraldsuites.com.

Emerald Suites provides fully furnished one and two-bedroom lodgings for an extended stay on the Las Vegas Strip in a non-gaming environment. Amenities include high-speed internet access, and fully equipped kitchens. Relax in the pool here or spend a night on the town with free tickets to Las Vegas shows.

Golden Nugget

$ –$$ **1,907 Rooms**
129 East Fremont St.
702-385-7111or 800-846-5336.
www.goldennugget.com.

Downtown's largest hotel was acquired by Landry's Restaurant Corp. in 2005 and given a $100 million redo that put sharks in the middle of the pool, new restaurants and lounges around the hotel, new softgoods in the rooms, new suites to reserve and a new VIP check-in area for those who want to pay a premium for more personalized service.

The hotel actually dates back to 1946 and has had several lives, including a 28-year run with Steve Wynn, who gave it a glamorous edge and brought entertainers like Frank Sinatra in to sing its praises. The property is still the crown of Downtown and the only local property with a full-service spa. You will find two Starbuck's within. Also a high stakes poker room, and a nightclub overlooking the promenade on Fremont St.

Golden Nugget

Las Vegas News Bureau/LVCVA

Hooters Casino Hotel

$ –$$ **696 Rooms**
115 E. Tropicana Ave.
702-739-9000 or 866-678-2582.
www.hchvegas.com.

If you like orange, look no further than Hooters, which labels itself "the cure for the common casino." Orange-flavored tank tops and hot pants abound. Even the rooms have orange trimmings. Where the Hooters girls leave off, the beach comes in and the hotel is themed throughout with surf and sand motifs. Rooms include a round bar table with orange bar stools, beds with 500 threadcount sheets and high-speed internet access (for a fee, of course). There's a casino, a 24-hour café with signature Buffalo Wings, entertainment and plenty of eye candy in this location across from the MGM Grand.

Imperial Palace Hotel & Casino

$ –$$ **2,700 Rooms**
3535 Las Vegas Blvd. S.
702-731-3311 or 800-634-6441.
www.imperialpalace.com.

There is more to this pagoda-roofed casino hotel than meets the eye. Although its casino is no match for the grandeur of the megaresorts, inside the hotel is a widespread complex with restaurants, an Olympic-size pool, a spa, a showroom where Legends in Concert (*see Great Imposters*) appears, and The Auto Collections of antique cars (*see Museums*). The deluxe rooms have recently been freshened with soothing neutral hues and all the standard amenities; high-speed wireless internet and in-room refrigerators are available for an additional fee. During the summer, the Imperial Palace hosts its celebrated Hawaiian luaus by the pool. Players will also get a kick out of the casino's "dealertainment" component that puts celebrity look-alikes in the pit.

JW Marriott

$ –$$ 541 Rooms
221 N. Rampart Blvd., Summerlin. 702-869-7777 or 877-869-8777. www.jwmarriottlv.com.

This upscale Marriott provides a refreshing way to enjoy Las Vegas, since it's located in the desert west of The Strip in the planned community of Summerlin. The 54-acre landscaped resort also has a casino, which offers customers plenty of fun promotions. Two six-story towers, designed in the style of a Mediterranean villa, offer large rooms with oversize bathrooms, walk-in closets, coffee-makers, cozy robes, powerful raindrop shower nozzles and—perhaps most important—plenty of peace and quiet. A 40,000sq ft spa adds to the relaxation as does the Marriott's exclusive relationship with nearby Tournament Players Club at the Canyons, a PGA Tour facility.

Renaissance Las Vegas

$ –$$ 548 Rooms & Suites
3400 Paradise Rd. 702-784-5700 or 800-750-0980. www.renaissance lasvegas.com.

Boutique by Las Vegas standards, this 14-story, 500-room hotel just east of The Strip delivers on convenience and class as a non-gaming (the city's largest) property. A two-story club level is worth the nominal investment for comfort, business, continental breakfast, snacks, (heavy) hors d' oeuvres, desserts and cocktails. Standard are the 300-threadcount Egyptian cotton bed linens, fluffy down comforter and duvet, flat-panel LCD HD television, in-room high-speed internet access and separate bath and shower. The dining experience at Envy Steakhouse is one of the city's best-kept secrets with an innovative menu and impressive wine list.

Silverton

$–$$ 300 rooms and suites
3333 Blue Diamond Rd. 702-263-7777 or 866-946-4373. www.silvertoncasino.com.

Located at the extended South end of The Strip, Silverton is especially popular with the driving crowd coming in from Los Angeles as it is located off the Interstate about three miles south of Mandalay Bay. Its 300 rooms keep an Adirondack lodge theme in place and the rooms were recently remodeled to keep it all fresh. The casino brings a 117,000-gal. aquarium with 4,000 frenzied fish. Add six dining venues and a warehouse-size Outdoor World shopping site and you have enough to keep you busy without even touching The Strip.

South Point Hotel, Casino & Spa

$ –$$ 1350 Rooms
9777 Las Vegas Blvd. South. 702-796-7111 or 866-796-7111. www.southpointcasino.com

The southernmost casino on The Strip (or just beyond it), the South

HOTELS

149

Point offers oversized rooms in a behemoth property that includes a a 64-lane bowling alley, as well as a massive BINGO hall, a 16-screen multiplex cinema, an equestrian arena, a spa, seven dining venues, a lagoon-shaped pool and wireless internet access. A full-service spa takes on the aches and pains of the guests- especially from the rodeo finalists during the annual NFR competitions.

Sunset Station

$ –$$ 457 Rooms
1301 W. Sunset Rd. at Stephanie St., Henderson. 702-547-7777, or 888-786-7389. www.sunsetstation.com.

This casino hotel, located just minutes from Lake Mead and Hoover Dam, brings a touch of the Mediterranean to the area with its Spanish-style architecture and colorful centerpiece Gaudi bar. In addition to its 3,000 slot and video-poker machines, Sunset Station books headliners at its 5,000-seat outdoor amphitheater. Dining options include several upscale restaurants and a food court.

Tuscany

$ –$$ All-Suites
255 E. Flamingo Rd. 702-893-8933 or 877-887-2261. www.tuscany lasvegas.com.

The suites here bring comfortable hotel-style décor with the amenities of in-room coffee makers (and complimentary coffee), dining areas and large refrigerators. This property reads more like a desert resort with a casino rather than a Las Vegas hotel. It has a meandering and nicely landscaped pool area, full service dining, a fitness

room, entertainment and a casino with a layout more fitting for a golf resort about a mile east of The Strip.

Westin Casuarina Las Vegas Hotel, Casino & Spa

$ –$$ 826 Rooms
160 E. Flamingo Rd. 702-836-5900 or 800-851-1703. www.westin.com.

On the site of the former Maxim Hotel, the Westin redo brings 816 contemporary guest rooms and 10 suites to the Vegas bed count-all equipped with Westin's signature plush Heavenly Bed, Heavenly Bath with dual shower heads, dual-line telephones and high-speed internet. Marble baths, fluffy duvets and terry cloth robes add extra elegance and comfort. The welcoming Hibiscus Spa is an added amenity, complete with a Vichey shower and 15 treatment rooms for facials, massages and body wraps. Wet and dry saunas, an outdoor Jacuzzi and a pool with private cabanas complete the experience. The hotel no longer permits smoking in the rooms or interior public areas –except for the casino and lounge.

Echo Bay Resort & Marina

$ –$$ 50 Rooms
On Lake Mead, in Overton. 702-394-4000 or 800-752-9669. www.echobay7c.com.

The whole family will have fun at this resort on the shores of Lake Mead—even Fido is welcome here. Using the comfortable hotel as a base, you can rent a houseboat, ski boat or other watercraft. The resort's adjacent RV park offers services that include laundry, showers and a restaurant.

HOTELS BY THEME

Looking for a hip hangout in Las Vegas or a quiet place off The Strip? Want a good bargain, or need a business hotel? In the preceding Pages, we've organized the properties by price category, so below we've broken them out by theme to help you plan your trip.

Best Bang for the Buck
Alexis Park Resort & Spa *(p 147)*
Artisan *(p 147)*
Echo Bay Resort & Marina *(p 150)*
Emerald Suites *(p 147)*
🛏 Golden Nugget *(p 147)*
Signature (p 146)
South Point *(p 149)*
Sunset Station *(p 150)*
Westin Casuarina *(p 150)*

For Business Travelers
Four Seasons
   Hotel Las Vegas *(p 144)*
Rio All-Suite Casino & Hotel *(p 146)*
🛏 Trump Las Vegas *(p 145)*
Westin Casuarina *(p 150)*

Hotels with Hip Décor
Artisan *(p 147)*
Hard Rock Hotel *(p 144)*
🛏 Skylofts *(p 144)*

Off The Strip
Artisan *(p 147)*
Alexis Park Resort & Spa *(p 147)*
Four Seasons Hotel *(p 144)*
🛏 Golden Nugget *(p 148)*
Hard Rock Hotel *(p 144)*
Westin Casuarina *(p 150)*

No Casino
Artisan *(p 147)*
Alexis Park Resort & Spa *(p 147)*
Four Seasons Hotel *(p 144)*
Emerald Suites *(p 147)*
Montelago Village Resort *(p 146)*
Ritz-Carlton Lake Las Vegas *(p 144)*
Signature *(p 146)*
🛏 Trump Las Vegas *(p 145)*

Spa Experiences
Alexis Park Resort & Spa *(p 147)*
Bally's Las Vegas *(p 145)*
Four Seasons Las Vegas *(p 144)*
🛏 Golden Nugget *(p 148)*
Imperial Palace
   Hotel & Casino *(p 148)*
Ritz-Carlton Lake Las Vegas *(p 144)*
🛏 Trump Las Vegas *(p 145)*
Westin Casuarina *(p 150)*

Vegas Classics
Alexis Park *(p 147)*
🛏 Golden Nugget *(p 148)*

Way Off The Strip
Echo Bay Resort & Marina *(p 150)*
🛏 Loews Lake
   Las VegasResort *(p 145)*
🛏 JW Marriott *(p 149)*
Montelago Village Resort *(p 146)*
Ritz-Carlton, Lake Las Vegas *(p 144)*
Sunset Station *(p 150)*

HOTELS

MICHELIN GUIDE

The Michelin Guide provides a comprehensive selection and rating of hotels and restaurants in all categories of comfort and prices. As part of our meticulous and highly confidential evaluation process, Michelin's American inspectors conducted anonymous visits to restaurants and hotels in Las Vegas. The following is a selection to suit all wallets, taken from the current edition. *Jean-Luc Naret, Director, Michelin Guides*

Restaurants

A number of things are judged when giving Michelin stars, including quality of ingredients, technical skill and flair in preparation, blend and clarity of flavors, the balance of the menu and the ability to produce excellent cooking time and again.

Cuisine	❀ to ❀❀❀
Comfort	✗ to ✗✗✗✗✗

DOWNTOWN

Andre's ❀ ✗✗
FRENCH
401 S. 6th St.
(bet. Bridger & Clark Aves.)
Phone: 702-385-5016
Web: www.andrelv.com
Prices: $$$$

Long before Las Vegas claimed a constellation of star chefs, Andre's was the city's special occasion restaurant. Tucked away on a quiet residential street, this 1930's-era home has been transformed into a warm, French provincial setting, with bottles from local icon, chef and owner André Rochat's private collection of Cognac and Armagnac displayed in the front reception and bar areas. French cuisine here excels in classicism, restraint and formality.

Vic & Anthony's ✗✗✗
STEAKHOUSE
129 Fremont St. (at 1st St.)
(in the Golden Nugget)
Phone: 702-386-8399
Web: www.vicandanthonys.com
Prices: $$$$

Downtown Las Vegas is steakhouse central, where every hotel seems to claim a restaurant honoring meat in its many forms. Vic & Anthony's fits the mould with its dark, clubby atmosphere, full of wood paneling, leather chairs and candlelight. Your satisfaction is the staff's command here. When servers bring your steak to the table, they will request that you cut into it to make sure that the meat is cooked to your liking. Who wouldn't like a juicy filet mignon, perfectly seared until the outside is crisp and the inside is tender and moist?

THE STRIP

Alex ❀❀ ✗✗✗✗✗
CONTEMPORARY
3131 Las Vegas Blvd. S.
(Wynn)
Phone: 702-7703300
Web: www.wynnlasvegas.com
Prices: $$$$

Alex is the kind of place you want to go to impress a date, pop an important question or wine and dine VIP clients. Who wouldn't be impressed descending the marble staircase into this comely room clad in soft flounces copper-colored draperies and lit by shimmering crystal chandeliers? Credit Alessandro Stratta's Italian-French heritage for inspiring the chef's refined cooking. "Rivier Cuisine," as the restaurant bills it, boils down to contemporary French food with a soupçon of Italian influence stirred in for good measure.

Isla 𝕏𝕏
MEXICAN
3300 Las Vegas Blvd. S. (TI)
Phone: 702-894-7349
Web: www.treasureisland.com
Prices: $$
Park your pirate ship outside and swagger on in to Isla. With lively Latin music, young, friendly servers, and a menu created by Mexico-born chef Richard Sandoval (of Pampano and Maya in New York City), Isla whips up good food and fun at Treasure Island. Enter through the tequila bar , where premium tequila is the quaff of choice —mixed into margaritas or enjoyed in a Goddess Elixir, prepared tableside by Isla's own sensual Tequila Goddess.
Several different types of guacamole are prepared tableside; try it with the grilled filet mignon with a cheese enchilada in mole sauce.

Joël Robuchon 🕸🕸🕸
CONTEMPORARY   𝕏𝕏𝕏𝕏
3799 Las Vegas Blvd. S.
(at the MGM Grand)
Phone: 702-891-7925
Web: www.mgmgrand.com
Prices: $$$$
Fashioned as an opulent Belle Époque salon, down to the last or-

nate wall molding, this restaurant feels miles away from the casino just outside the doors. Settle into a purple velvet banquette or a table in the landscaped indoor garden, and the world simply melts away. Prepare to experience perfection on a plate. Celebrated chef Joël Robuchon, who came out of retirement a few years ago, is now an integral part of the Vegas fine-dining arena. Presented with striking visual effect, his transcendent dishes (as in pan-seared seabass with lemongrass foam or truffle velouté on celeriac custard with sweet onion) find inspiration through the regions of France. A meal here is an event, during which you will progress through a series of courses, beginning with a tableau of artisan breads and ending with a palette of jewel-like miniature pastries, jellies and chocolates.

Picasso 🕸🕸   𝕏𝕏𝕏𝕏𝕏
MEDITERRANEAN
3600 Las Vegas Blvd. S.
(Bellagio)
Phone: 702-693-7223
Web: www.bellagio.com
Prices: $$$$
Take the name literally. Set about with original paintings and ceramics by the restaurant's namesake artist, as well as stylish carpeting and furniture designed by Pablo's son, Claude, Picasso gives a new meaning to the art of dining. While the dining.room's floor-to-ceiling windows look out at more than 1,00 fountains that perform a dazzling spectacle of water and light at regular intervals, the view can't begin to compete with the stunning – and priceless – artwork inside. Spanish-born

RESTAURANTS

chef Julian Serrano, who has been the master of Picasso's kitchen since it opened in 1998, paints his epicurean canvas with broad, well-executed strokes. Flavors of Spain and France color the cuisine in two different tasting menus featuring thoughtfully composed dishes and presentation.

Social House ※※
ASIAN

3300 Las Vegas Blvd. S. (at TI)
Phone: 702-894-7777
Web: www.socialhouselv.com
Prices: $$$

Come graze with the glitterati at TI's new 'it' restaurant. Take the elevator or climb the stairway lined with metal safe-deposit-like boxes to reach this oh-so-hip second-floor haunt. The place is a bit schizophrenic, as if it can't decide between being a nightclub or a restaurant. And so it does both; DJs spin tunes each evening, and dining tables morph into conveyances for cocktails with the help of a hydraulic system. As expensive as it is expansive, the menu rolls out sushi and sashimi along with the likes of Kob beef three ways and citrus peel miso-marinated cod. Snag a seat on the outdoor patio for a front-row seat for the provocative Sirens of TI show.

Top of the World ※※
AMERICAN

2000 Las Vegas Blvd. S. (Stratosphere)
Phone: 702-380-7711
Web: www.topoftheworldlv.com
Prices: $$$

Acrophobics need not apply at this lofty restaurant, which looms 832 feet in the air at the top of the Stratosphere Tower. But if you crave an unparalleled 360-degree view of The Strip in all its glittering glory, you've come to the right place. A full revolution takes about an hour and twenty minutes. Don't expect the food to match the height of the tower, though; this is a place where view definitely trumps cuisine.

Valentino ※※※
ITALIAN

3355 Las Vegas Blvd. S.
(at the Venetian)
Phone: 702-414-3000
Web: www.valentinolv.com
Prices: $$$$

Sister to Valentino in Los Angeles, the Santa Monica stalwart of Sicilian-born restaurateur Piero Selvaggio for more than 30 years, this version debuted on the Vegas Strip in 1998. Inside, the boisterous and casual grill gives way to the more refined dining rooms beyond, which received a recent redesign in tones of teal with copper accents. Executive chef/partner Luciano Pellegrini commands the kitchen, improvising his creative takes on pasta and gnocchi, as well as roasted branzino, and Kobe-style beef braised in Barolo.

Wing Lei ※ ※※※※
CHINESE

3131 Las Vegas Blvd. S.
Phone: 702-248-3463
Web: www.wynnlasvegas.com
Prices: $$$$

In keeping with the sumptuous tone of the Wynn resort, Wing Lei dresses in Imperial splendor Abalone, mother-of-pearl and 14-carat gold accent the opulent room, while windows peer out on a black marble Botero sculpture flanked by 100-year-old pomegranate trees. A native of Taiwan, chef Richard Chen entices diner with his haute Chinese cuisine. Using a "reverse fusion" technique, the chef evokes the seasons with dishes such as a beautifully balanced and composed salad of peekytoe crab, diced avocado and sweet mango.

WEST OF THE STRIP

Ferraro's ✗✗
ITALIAN
5900 W. Flamingo Rd.
(bet Decatur & Jones Blvds.)
Phone: 702-364-5300
Web: www.ferraroslasvegas.com
Prices: $$

Finally, an off-strip restaurants that's not located in a strip mall. This stand-alone structure on Flamingo Road welcomes diners with true Italian warmth. That's not surprising, since the elegant eatery has been run by the Ferraro family since 1985. These days Mimmo Ferraro holds the reins in the kitchen. Here he maintains the family's commitment to tradition, serving up the signature osso buco, along with homemade pastas, market-fresh seafood and *festa* Ferraro for two (a hearty meat sauce made with spare ribs, meat-balls and sausage), accompanied by a mainly Italian and Californian winelists. Most customers are regulars, drawn by the genial staff, well-spaced tables, cozy booths and serious cooking.

Ping Pang Pong ✗
CHINESE
4000 W. Flamingo Rd.
(at the Gold Coast Las Vegas)
Phone: 702-247-8136
Web: www.goldcoastcasino.com
Prices: $

It's an intriguing name suggesting a one-off table tennis game to English speakers, but the food her is no joke. Housed inside the un-pretentious Gold Coast Hotel, this popular place spotlights speciali-ties from the diverse provinces of China. The menu wanders through noodles and rice to clay pot dishes and congee, and from tea-smoke duck to whole-steamed fish. Locals flock at lunch time for dim sum. Ping Pang Pong is a bargain, with a dim sum lunch or an average three-course dinner will cost you only just shy of $25.

EAST OF THE STRIP

Medici Cafe ✗✗✗
CONTEMPORARY
1610 Lake Las Vegas Pkwy.,
Henderson (in the Ritz-Carlton)
Phone: 702-567-4700
Web: www.ritzcarlton.com
Prices: $$$

Housed in the Ritz Carlton Lake Las Vegas, Medici Café visually lives up to its noble Tuscan name. The lovely terrace looks onto the hotel's Florentine garden, while Italianate furnishings and reproductions of Renaissance art grace the interior. More a princely dining retreat than a formal hall, the space is just right for another kind of renaissance, which is re-flected in the display kitchen and its ambitious contemporary menu. Reviving classic American fare like pan-roasted chicken doesn't pre-vent the kitchen from venturing abroad, however, especially back to the Mediterranean: Pan-roasted halibut is accented with saffron, basil and preserved lemon. Save room for the signature chocolate soufflé.

RESTAURANTS

155

Hotels

While The Strip offers an unending catwalk of sizzling new rooms, suites and entertainment options – often for premium advances from your pocket – there are plenty of properties near The Strip that proffer some hot action of their own in sprawling settings and comely spaces that boast a fraction of The Strip's blistering rates. Those listed here are from the most recent edition of the Michelin Guide to Las Vegas.

Comfort to

THE STRIP

Monte Carlo
2743 Rooms/259 Suites
3770 Las Vegas Blvd. S. (bet. Harmon & Tropicana Aves.)
Phone: 702-730-7777
Web: www.montecarlo.com
Prices: $$
Set back from the boulevard, the Monte Carlo evoked as undersated elegance compared to more flamboyant strip properties. The refined image will hit home when you enter the marble-lined lobby, hung with crystal chandeliers and adorned with potted palms. It will be reinforced if you dine at Andre's (*see Michelin Guide Restaurants*), which is decked out like a French château. This hotel boasts just over 3,000 guest rooms, newly renovated with contemporary fittings, complete with flat-screen TVs and high-speed internet access. Suites add amenities such as dining rooms, wet bars, remote control lighting, marble bathrooms, steam showers and whirlpool tubs.

EAST OF THE STRIP

Green Valley Ranch
490 Rooms
2300 Paseo Verde Dr. (at I-215), Henderson105 E. Harmon Ave. (bet. Audrie St.& Las Vegas
Phone: 702-617-7777
Web: www.greenvalleyranch resort.com
Prices: $$
You won't miss out on the action at Green Valley Ranch. Located 7 miles east of The Strip via I-215, this Mediterranean style resort has it all: a casino, a 10,000sq ft European day spa, a cinema complex, even a working vineyard. Spacious, plush rooms are divided between the East and West towers. Dark wood furnishings hold up the ritzy feel, while large windows look out over surrounding mountains. 'Main Street' shops and restaurants are out front, while the 'backyard' has an 8-acre pool complex with a sand beach. Shuttles run to the airport and The Strip.

Las Vegas Hilton
2833 Rooms/124 Suites
3000 Paradise Rd. (bet. Convention Center Dr. & Karen Ave.)
Phone: 702-732-5111
Web: www.lvhilton.com
Prices: $$
Convenient to the Las Vegas Convention Center, the Hilton claims the distinction of having hosted Elvis Presley's Sin City debut in July 1969, when the hotel was known as the International. Vegas glitz is in short supply here, rooms are basic and conservative and you won't get the type of service you'd be treated to at a swankier Strip hotel. Nevertheless, the hotel has decent amenities for the price,

including outdoor pool, fitness center, spa, salon, putting green and a video arcade.

Platinum 🏨

255 Suites
211 E. Flamingo Rd. (at Koval Ln.)
Phone: 702-365-5000
Web: www.theplatinumhotel.com
Prices: $$

If gambling's not your cup of tea, you'll find this non-gaming, non-smoking, all-suites hotel to be right up your quiet alley. Services and amenities include an indoor/outdoor pool, a state-of-the-art fitness center, a noteworthy restaurant (*see Restaurants*) and 4,000sq ft WELL spa. The residential atmosphere is couched in three tiers of spacious suites, with gourmet kitchens, Bose sound systems, outdoor terraces and whirlpool tubs; larger suites get fireplaces, washers and dryers. The Strip is only two blocks away.

DOWNTOWN

Main Street Station 🏨

406 Rooms/14 Suites
200 N. Main St. (at Stewart Ave.)
Phone: 702-387-1896
Web: www.mainstreetcasino.com
Prices: $

Victorian-era civility lives on at Main Street Station. Located just a few blocks away from the computer-generated sound and light show known as the Fremont Street Experience, this casino cashes in on the ambience of a bygone era. Renovated rooms are contemporary, while common areas feature period antiques and vintage Pullman railroad cars. Trains whistling by on the active tracks nearby only add to the railroad theme.

WEST OF THE STRIP

Orleans 🏨

1867 rooms/19 suites
4500 W. Tropicana Ave. (at Arville St.)
Phone: 702-365-7111
Web: www.orleanscasino.com
Prices: $

With its lively French Quarter theme, the Orleans provides comfortable, quiet and well-maintained rooms that don't skimp on size with 450sq ft as the standard. Complementary valet parking and free shuttles to The Strip are among the more attractive amenities. The Orleans is known for its 70-lane bowling center and the 9,000-seat Orleans Arena next door, which hosts everything from monster-truck rallies to championship boxing matches to the circus. In the hotel's showroom you can catch music acts and comedians, or instead just head for the spa or the pool.

Red Rock Resort 🏨

814 Rooms/45 Suites
11011 W. Charleston Blvd. (at I-215)
Phone: 702-797-7777
Web: www.redrocklasvegas.com
Prices: $$$

One of the city's newest resorts, this sophisticated retreat flaunts its enviable setting near Red Rock Canyon National Conservation Area. The spa uses the park as a playground, offering a full menu of kayak and bike tours, hiking and horseback riding, and rock climbing and river rafting. The lobby drips with inlaid marble and cascading crystal chandeliers, while zebra-striped wood paneling and modern art adorn the hallways. Rooms are spacious and contemporary with floor-to-ceiling windows.

HOTELS

LAS VEGAS

The following abbreviations may appear in this Index: NHS National Historic Site; NM National Monument; NMem National Memorial; NP National Park; NHP National Historical Park; NRA National Recreational Area; NWR National Wildlife Refuge; SP State Park; SHP State Historical Park; SHS State Historic Site.

List of Maps